The Transformative Daf

MOSAICA PRESS

RABBI DANIEL FRIEDMAN

The Transformative Daf

Tractate Rosh Hashanah

Published by Mosaica Press, Inc.
www.mosaicapress.com
info@mosaicapress.com

Dedication

have been privileged to sponsor many Jewish publications and in the course of so doing, I have honoured my family, living and deceased, many times, so I really consider this one a gift to myself on the occasion, later this year, of my 75th birthday, and I offer my heartfelt gratitude to the Almighty for all his multiple blessings, not least allowing me to reach this venerable age in good condition.

Nevertheless, I cannot lose the opportunity of mentioning at least a few people who were, or are, very dear to me.

Those who are no longer with us:

My beloved friend for over forty years, **Sam Peltz**, whom I miss terribly.

My friend and partner, **Larry Adler**, who helped me succeed and who was the source of such wise counsel.

My childhood companion with whom I grew up and was always in contact, **Martin Jaskel**.

My **Uncle Freddy Danzig**, my childhood hero, and **Auntie Lydia**, who kept the past alive for so long.

My sparring partner, **Rabbi Jonathan Sacks**, in recognition of his unique contribution to the Jews of his generation, which I am sure will continue to be recognised by future generations.

My one and only boss, **Alec and Eileen Colman**. "I kept my promise."

On a happier note, those whom I can still enjoy:

Gabi and Gina Katri, who sealed my life's fulfilment when they made the shidduch with Danielle.

Jonathan and Andrea Lass. Jonathan, since the first day at UCS 15/9/1959 and as a couple when we both married in 1985, 36 years ago.

Our New York Shabbat families for more years than I can remember, **Muk and Vivien Eisenman** and **Shalom and Wendy Greenbaum**.

David and Joyce Muller, a unique multi (5) generation friendship originating more than 120 years ago when David's great-grandfather was the doctor who delivered my dear father and his brothers in what was then Czechoslovakia.

Danny and Helen Dover, who have played an important role in our lives.

Rabbi David and Rebbetzin Devorah Refson, for decades of loving friendship.

My brother- and sister-in-law and their children and grandchildren, **Eli and Lulu Arazi**, a model of Jewish family life.

I met **Rabbi Daniel Friedman** and his **Rebbetzin Batya** at the bat mitzvah of the youngest daughter of Tim and Sasha Bolot. I was Tim's *sandek*, and his father, Peter, and late mother, Sandra, were friends from 1966. Rabbi Daniel and Batya made an immediate impression on me, and it is with gratitude and pleasure that I am associated with what I am sure will be a seminal contribution to Jewish learning.

Michael M H Gross

BETH DIN ZEDEK
ECCLESIASTICAL JUDICATURE OF THE
CHICAGO RABBINICAL COUNCIL

בית דין צדק דק"ק שיקגו והגליל
דמועצת הרבנים דשיקגו

בס"ד

הרב גדלי' דוב שווארץ זצ"ל, ראב"ד מלפנים
RABBI GEDALIA DOV SCHWARTZ *of blessed memory*
Rosh Beth Din Emeritus

הרב ישראל מאיר קרנו זצ"ל, ראב"ד מלפנים
RABBI ISRAEL M. KARNO *of blessed memory*
Av Beth Din Emeritus

הרב חיים דוד רגנשברג זצ"ל, מייסד חבד"ץ
RABBI C. DAVID REGENSBERG *of blessed memory*

הרב יונה ריס, אב"ד
RABBI YONA REISS
Av Beth Din

הרב אברהם מרדכי אברמסון
RABBI ALAN M. ABRAMSON
Menahel

כ"ד לסדר אמור אל הכהנים ותשפ"א

בנפש נאמן.

Our esteemed colleague Rabbi Daniel Friedman שליט"א has written a lucid and lyrical book, Daf Yomi, that extracts nuggets of wisdom and pearls of perspicacity from the pages of the Talmud. As an experienced and successful shul Rabbi, Rabbi Friedman has a special talent for connecting with his audience, whether through the written word or the spoken sermon, in a fashion which is (כמאמרם ז"ל) משיב נפש, capable of restoring a persons spititual well-being, and intellectual appreciation of the Torah's values and teachings. One cannot help but be enriched by Rabbi Friedmans combination of psychological acuity, human compassion, and religious fervor.

וזכי' אבותינו הגדול הנ"ל, שיזכה להגדיל תורה ולהאדיר ברבים,

בברכת וידידות,

Yona Reiss

2701 W. Howard Street, Chicago, Illinois 60645-1303
Phone & Fax: 1-773-250-5482   bethdin@crcweb.org

מוסדות אור שמח מרכז טננבאום ע.ר. 00-21343-00-58
רח׳ שמעון הצדיק 22-28 ירושלים ת.ד. 18103
טל: 0315-581-02
Nissan 5781

MICHTAV BRACHA

Chazal say, "Great is learning because it leads to [virtuous] action" (*Kiddushin* 40b). Ramban writes in his celebrated letter that after learning anything in Torah, one should seek some way to apply that teaching to one's life. Every part of Hashem's Torah is precious beyond measure, but many, perhaps most, of us have some difficulty finding this application. While there are many passages in Tanach and Talmud where the practical lessons are clear, with many others, the message is obscure and elusive.

Rabbi Daniel Friedman has performed a truly valuable service in providing some badly needed assistance. He has authored a book going through the 2,700 plus pages of the Babylonian Talmud, extracting from each *daf* lessons that can be applied to real life. Some stress practical behavior, such as fixing negative character traits and acquiring and developing virtuous ones, others are inspirational, and still others provide a broader philosophical perspective that can help us in our life's journey to become true *avdei Hashem*. Those who study the *daf yomi* will walk away with practical guidance that will elevate the *ruchniyus* in their lives; for those who do not yet study the *daf*, there is the additional benefit of giving them a way to participate in this wonderful global learning endeavor.

Rabbi Friedman deserves our heartfelt gratitude for producing a work that is so helpful on both a practical and inspirational level. May he have much *hatzlachah* both in the dissemination of this book and in all of his *avodas ha'kodesh*.

With Torah blessings,
Yitzchak A. Breitowitz
Rav, Kehillat Ohr Somayach, Yerushalayim

Table of Contents

Preface

Following an *aliyah* to the Torah, we bless Hashem: "Who has given us a Torah of truth and secured everlasting life within us." The *Tur*[1] explains the *berachah*: "Torah of truth" refers to *Torah She'bichsav*, the Written Torah, while "And secured everlasting life within us" refers to *Torah She'baal Peh*, the Oral Torah. Our primary repository of *Torah She'baal Peh* is the Babylonian Talmud, known simply as the Gemara, meaning "learning." While we have poured over the Gemara throughout our history, a revolution in daily Talmud study took place a century ago. Rabbi Meir Shapiro of Lublin created a learning program called "*daf yomi*," whereby every person around the world would learn the same page of Gemara daily. After seven-and-a-half years, all 2,711 pages would be studied. What began with a modest following has now become a movement with hundreds of thousands of devotees worldwide.

And yet for many, *daf yomi* remains an enigma. Some have attempted and not connected with the pace. Others don't feel capable of the level of intensity demanded by the magnitude of the task. And then there are those who do learn the *daf* but live with a constant internal struggle over whether, given daily time constraints, there may be other *sefarim* they should consider learning.

---

1   *Tur, Orach Chaim* 139.

The goal of *The Transformative Daf* is to address all of these issues. For some people, this *sefer* offers the opportunity to connect with the *daf yomi* movement—to learn something each day from the *daf* while not covering the entire page. It's about joining the conversation. It's about talking about the *daf* with your spouse and children, your friends in shul, and your colleagues at work. It means never being short of a conversation-starter or a *d'var Torah* about *inyanei d'yoma*, matters of the day.

The Transformative Daf is not just for those who don't learn the full *daf*. It's very much designed as well for people who learn the *daf* and want to walk away with something practical for daily living. The purpose is to answer the question: Now that you've learned the *daf*, how will your day and your life be transformed for the better? As we declare in the *berachah* after an *aliyah*, Hashem has secured everlasting life within us. Where? In the Gemara. Everlasting doesn't only mean the afterlife. It includes right here, right now, your life today.

Every page of the Gemara, every line, every word, and every letter contain the secrets of the universe to achieving everlasting life. If we don't see it, it means we haven't delved deep enough; we haven't worked hard enough. The answers are all there. It's our task to decipher the message by our "toil in it day and night." *The Transformative Daf* is merely a small attempt at understanding the messages secured in the words of our holy Torah. One message each day; a tiny contribution to a boundless conversation.

The lessons each day are derived from the words of our Sages throughout the generations. Wherever I have found commentary on the *daf*, I have devoted my best efforts to anchoring each idea in earlier teachings of the traditional *mefarshim*. Where I have struggled with the meaning and message, I have davened for *siyata d'Shmaya* that my suggested explanations align with our *mesorah* and find favor in Hashem's eyes. I thank Rabbi M. Sussman for your incredible assistance in amending and fine-tuning many of the ideas. I take complete and sole responsibility for any pieces remaining with unresolved *mesorah* difficulties and will endeavor to correct such missteps in future editions. To that end, I welcome the feedback of those learning *The Transformative Daf*.

The Transformative Daf series is beginning with *Rosh Hashanah*. That was not always the intention, but Hakadosh Baruch Hu decides these things. It is, of course, very appropriate to be starting with this particular *masechta*. Rosh Hashanah is about new beginnings. Moreover, as we shall see in the first lesson, people have a tendency to wait until the "perfect time" to renew their commitment to Torah and mitzvos. But the perfect time is now. *Rosh* means head. *Shanah* means change. There's no better place to begin than the tractate that calls upon us to change our mindset; to transform how we think and behave as we go about our daily lives. *Rosh Hashanah* is the perfect *masechta* to begin *The Transformative Daf*.

While the Almighty directs the world in these uncanny and extraordinary ways, we must nonetheless acknowledge what is happening from our perspective. And so, the *daas tachton* reason for the series beginning at *Rosh Hashanah* is the vision of an incredible supporter of Torah, Michael Gross. As a result of Michael's encouragement and generosity, a project that originated as a daily online teaching is now being "transformed" into a *sefer*, amplifying the message of the *daf* far and wide. In the *zechus* of this mitzvah, may you and Danielle have only good health, continued spiritual and material prosperity, and unlimited *nachas* from your children and grandchildren till 120.

There are many other people without whom this *sefer* would not have been possible. First and foremost, to my dear wife and soulmate, Rabbanit Batya Yocheved, who has been a constant source of inspiration, guidance, and patience over the many years of *The Transformative Daf* thus far; words cannot express my eternal gratitude to Hashem for the *basherte* He has given me. And my appreciation likewise goes to our five wonderful daughters, Miriam Leah, Sarah Joar, Yemima Chana, Ella Bracha, and Levana Rivka, for all your patience with Abba's writing. Thank you to my parents, Ben and Eve Friedman, of Sydney, Australia, and in-laws, Yosef David and Sylvia Ivry, of New York, for always being there for us; we feel very blessed.

Thank you to Rabbis JJ Schacter, Yona Reiss, Daniel Korobkin, and Jonathan Gross, for your support and advice over the years. And a special tribute to Rav Gedalia Dov Schwartz, *zt"l*.

Thank you to Rabbis Yaacov Haber and Doron Kornbluth and the team at Mosaica Press for going above and beyond every step of the way. And I want to thank all those who have been on this journey with me from the days of Life Yomi to Daf Yo.Me to its current iteration. Your encouragement and engagement have helped me persevere day-in day-out over the last seven years.

Finally, thank you to the Ribbono Shel Olam for all the blessings in my life. I feel very humbled to be the vehicle for these teachings.

Rabbi Daniel Friedman
Iyar 5781
London

Shanah Tovah! Happy New Year!

The Almighty is about to deliver one of the most important messages that He has ever given to man. Now's the moment when He will establish an eternal covenant with Avraham's family for all eternity. He will reveal to Avraham the sojourn of his descendants and the ensuing salvation. He will promise him the land of Canaan as an inheritance for his offspring.

He tells Avraham to prepare for the historic conversation by gathering a number of animals and birds to be offered before God. Avraham obeys the instructions he receives to the very last detail.

And then, all of a sudden, he is overtaken by a deep slumber.

How could Avraham fall asleep upon such a momentous occasion?

מתני׳ אַרְבָּעָה רָאשֵׁי שָׁנִים הֵם בְּאֶחָד בְּנִיסָן רֹאשׁ הַשָּׁנָה לַמְּלָכִים וְלָרְגָלִים בְּאֶחָד בֶּאֱלוּל רֹאשׁ הַשָּׁנָה לְמַעְשַׂר בְּהֵמָה רַבִּי אֶלְעָזָר וְרַבִּי שִׁמְעוֹן אוֹמְרִים בְּאֶחָד בְּתִשְׁרֵי בְּאֶחָד בְּתִשְׁרֵי רֹאשׁ הַשָּׁנָה לַשָּׁנִים וְלַשְּׁמִיטִין וְלַיּוֹבְלוֹת לַנְטִיעָה וְלִירָקוֹת בְּאֶחָד בִּשְׁבָט רֹאשׁ הַשָּׁנָה לָאִילָן כְּדִבְרֵי בֵּית שַׁמַּאי בֵּית הִלֵּל אוֹמְרִים בַּחֲמִשָּׁה עָשָׂר בּוֹ:

There are four Rosh Hashanahs. The first of Nissan is the New Year for kings and festivals. The first of Elul is the New Year for tithing animals; Rabbi Elazar and Rabbi Shimon say: the first of Tishrei. The first of Tishrei is the New Year for years, Sabbatical years, Jubilee years, planting, and tithing vegetables. The first

of Shevat is the New Year for trees, according to Beis Shammai;
Beis Hillel says: on the fifteenth of the month.

How many people observe all of these Rosh Hashanahs? Most of us are familiar with the big one—the first of Tishrei. Some people might also celebrate the New Year for trees. Most people haven't even heard of the four New Years, let alone celebrate them. Why do we need multiple Rosh Hashanahs? Why could they not simply be rolled into one?

Remember those New Year's resolutions you made last Rosh Hashanah? Perhaps they lasted two weeks. For those more dedicated, maybe even a month or two before it was back to our old habits. It's not that we forgot about them completely; they're still lingering somewhere in the back of our mind. But, we tell ourselves that next Rosh Hashanah is only a few months away. Hopefully, we'll be able to try to start fresh then and get our good intentions back on track.

This Mishnah offers a powerful lesson about our New Year's resolutions. The next Rosh Hashanah isn't eleven months away. It's right around the corner! We don't have just one Rosh Hashanah per year. We have multiple opportunities to turn over a new leaf and start afresh!

Which is the first Rosh Hashanah mentioned in the Mishnah? Not the one we're all familiar with; that only makes it into third place. The first one, the first of Nissan, is the day Moshe and Aharon were instructed with the very first mitzvah given to our people. "This month is for you the head of the months. It is the first for you."

The *Sefas Emes* quotes the blessing that we recite daily prior to the *Shema*, which says that the Almighty "renews with His goodness *each day constantly* the works of creation." The word for month in Hebrew is *chodesh*, which is a form of the word *chadash*, meaning "new," on account of the renewal of the moon each month. The first mitzvah is to recognize that God renews us on a daily basis. That, says the *Sefas Emes*, is a fundamental tenet of our belief. That's why Nissan is the first Rosh Hashanah.[1]

---

1   *Sefas Emes, Likkutim, Mikeitz.*

Let's take a closer look at the words of the prayer. We bless God for renewing His goodness "each day constantly." If Hashem renews His works of creation constantly, what is the meaning of the daily renewal?

Here's where we need Avraham's slumber to explain things. Sleep is one of the greatest blessings Hashem has given us—not only because it refreshes us and endows us with renewed energy, but due to its line-drawing nature. Yesterday was yesterday; today is a new day with new potential. The period of slumber draws a line between whatever happened in the past and the exciting future that lies ahead. A reawakening is almost like a rebirth.

For Hashem, renewal occurs continuously. But, from our limited perspective, it's impossible to discern the difference between the present moment and two minutes earlier. It all appears to be one long flow of interrupted time. But then, Hashem gives us a gift to distinguish between moments in time. It's called the difference between yesterday and today.

Strictly speaking, just as one minute flows uninterruptedly into the next, similarly, one day flows straightforwardly into the next. But practically, we don't experience that smooth flow because the transition is disrupted by our slumber. And so, the clearest way to demonstrate Hashem's constant recreation from our perspective is the concept of daily renewal.

Why did Hashem send Avraham to sleep right when He wanted to reveal the unique purpose and mission of his family? That slumber represented a clean break with his past. He was no longer Avram of Ur Kasdim. Henceforth, he would be Avraham of the Promised Land. Hashem had recreated him.

You don't have to wait until the big Rosh Hashanah to experience the New Year. You don't even need to wait until one of the additional Rosh Hashanahs. Every day is a mini-Rosh Hashanah! It's a day of renewal when you can put the past behind you and turn over a new leaf.

Why is Rosh Hashanah called the "head of the year," as opposed to the "new year" or the "beginning of the year?" Our Sages explain that just like the head is the control center for the body, similarly Rosh Hashanah is the control center for the entire year. Your actions on Rosh Hashanah will determine your fate for the coming year. And so, we maximize our dedication to *"teshuvah, tefillah, u'tzedakah*—repentance, prayer, and charity," so that we are signed and sealed for a great year.

But really, every day is the control center for the days that follow it. To use an old cliché, today is the first day of the rest of your life. The decisions you make today will affect the rest of your life. If today you commit to becoming a better person, your entire life going forward will be changed for the better.

Shanah means year. But it's also related to the word *shoneh*, meaning different. Today is a new and different day to yesterday. As of today, your entire life, should you choose, could be different. Wishing you *"Shanah Tovah."* May today be the most important and impactful day of your life!

DAF 3

It's a Sign!

t's time for Yitzchak to get married. Avraham calls over his trusty aide, Eliezer, and instructs him to return to his birthplace to find a bride from his tribe. Eliezer sets out on his journey to Charan with a convoy of camels laden with gifts for Avraham's future daughter-in-law and *mechutanim*.

He arrives in Charan and rests by the well. How would he find a bride for Yitzchak? After pondering the matter, he devises a plan. "All the maidens are coming out to draw water," he says to himself. "I shall ask for a drink. If the girl responds with an offer not only to give me to drink but also to tend to my camels, that's a sign that she's the right girl for Yitzchak."

Almost magically, Rivkah appears and responds to Eliezer's request, just as he had hoped for. Eliezer had found the one!

But was it right of him to conjure up a "sign" to divine his way to Rivkah?

וַיִּשְׁמַע הַכְּנַעֲנִי מֶלֶךְ עֲרָד מָה שְׁמוּעָה שָׁמַע שָׁמַע שֵׁמַת אַהֲרֹן וְנִסְתַּלְקוּ עַנְנֵי כָּבוֹד וּכְסָבוּר נִיתְּנָה רְשׁוּת לְהִלָּחֵם בְּיִשְׂרָאֵל וְהַיְינוּ דִּכְתִיב (במדבר כ, כט) וַיִּרְאוּ כָּל הָעֵדָה כִּי גָוַע אַהֲרֹן וְאָמַר רַבִּי אַבָהוּ אַל תִּקְרֵי וַיִּרְאוּ אֶלָּא וַיִּירָאוּ.

"And the Canaanite, the king of Arad, heard [...and he waged war against Israel]." What report did he hear? He heard that Aharon had died and that the Clouds of Glory had withdrawn, and he thought that permission had been granted to wage war against the Jewish People. And this is the meaning of the verse,

5

> "And all the congregation saw that Aharon died." Rabbi Avohu
> said: Do not read it, "And they saw [va'yiru]"; rather, "And
> they were seen [va'yeira'u]" (by others, because the cover of the
> clouds of glory had been removed from them).

For forty years, the Children of Israel wandered through the wilderness. But far from being a perilous sojourn, they were living under the ever-watchful eye of our Father in Heaven. Their bread arrived daily on their doorstep—manna from Heaven. Their water was provided from the traveling Well of Miriam. And in Aharon the High Priest's merit, they were surrounded by the Clouds of Glory, guarding them from enemy attack and protecting them from the elements and other hazards.

But then, Aharon dies and the Clouds of Glory disappear. The wicked King of Arad takes it as a sign from Heaven that it is a propitious moment to attack Israel. He ambushes them, taking spoils of battle. The Israelites fight back and, with Hashem's help, are victorious.

Arad's animosity toward the Children of Israel had deep roots. His Amalekite army was the first to wage war against our people following the Exodus from Egypt. They were vanquished then but never lost sight of their desire to retaliate against the Israelites for their humiliating defeat. They waited forty years for the right time to strike.

All they needed was a sign.

The disappearance of the famed Clouds of Glory was a clear indication that their time had finally come. So, they gathered the troops and pounced.

Was it really a sign though? Or was it merely a crutch upon which to lean their wicked ambitions?

The Almighty sends us signs throughout our life to remind us that He's watching over us and pointing us in the right direction. It might be what seems like a little "coincidence" or a book that just happened to open up to a page with a pointed message. Our Father in Heaven encourages us and gives us hope with little signposts and banners along the way. According to the *Shach*, they're actually a form of mini-prophecy.[1]

---

1   *Shach, Yoreh De'ah* 179:5.

The more you place your trust in Hashem and align your life with His will, the more He will give you pointers along the way through life.

It's important, however, not to get led astray by false signs. Sometimes, we want something so bad that we convince ourselves that we're seeing a sign, when really, it's nothing more than an excuse to justify the decisions that we've already made. That's what occurred to the King of Arad. Was God sending him a sign—"giving him permission"—to strike the Israelites? Of course not. But, when we're looking for signs to support our preconceived decisions, it's not difficult to interpret what we see as Heavenly messages.

So, how do you know what's a real sign from God and what's a false sign? How do you distinguish between a prophetic nudge and the manipulations of the Satan?

God won't send you a sign to do the wrong thing. He has given you the incredible blessing of free will and a soul to make the right choice. So, if you think that you are seeing a sign to do the wrong thing, it's not a sign from God; it's a test to see whether you'll make the right choice.

The Almighty wants you to make a rational decision using your gift of free choice. Making life decisions based on your daily horoscope or random things that happen in your life is not what He wants. He wants you to place your life in His hand and be wholehearted with Him.

You should only run with a sign once you have made your own decision completely and rationally, and for the right reasons. At that point, if Hashem sends you a sign, it is a mark of His approval, a confirmation and embrace for having made the right choice. Signs are His way of smiling down and shining His countenance upon you.

Eliezer knew that the right girl for Yitzchak would be the one who exhibited exemplary kindness. That's the kind of person he was looking for. A sign would be the Divine stamp that he'd made the right calculation.[2]

May you give every option due consideration and make the sensible and pious choices in life, and may the Almighty provide you with the signs confirming you have made the right decision!

---

2   *Malbim, Bereishis* 24:14.

Making Deals with God

Y aakov has just escaped the wrath of his brother, Eisav. He is now on his way to Uncle Lavan and is fearful of what lies ahead. Hashem appears to him in a dream and assures him that He will protect him and bring him back to the Promised Land, a land that will be granted to Yaakov's future offspring.

Yaakov awakens from this powerful vision and vows: "If God shall be with me and protect me on this journey that I am embarking upon, giving me bread to eat and clothing to wear...everything You give me, I shall surely tithe unto you!"

That was quite a bold declaration on our forefather's part. Was he allowed to condition his tithes on the Almighty's protection? Is it OK to bargain with Heaven?

וְהָתַנְיָא הָאוֹמֵר סֶלַע זוֹ לִצְדָקָה בִּשְׁבִיל שֶׁיִּחְיוּ בָּנַי וּבִשְׁבִיל שֶׁאֶזְכֶּה בָּהּ לְחַיֵּי הָעוֹלָם הַבָּא הֲרֵי זֶה צַדִּיק גָּמוּר.

One who says, "I am giving this money to charity in order (bishvil) that my children should live or in order (bishvil) that I merit life in Olam Haba (Heaven)" is completely righteous.

Regarding the obligation to contribute gifts to the needy from one's produce, the Torah says, "*Aser te'aser.*"[1] The double-expression is usually

---

1   *Devarim* 14:22.

translated as, "You shall *surely* tithe." But the same expression was first used by Yaakov, meaning that there must be some additional layer of meaning to the phrase. Our Sages explain that it is an allusion to the idea that giving tzedakah leads to creating wealth. Here's how we should understand the verse: *"Aser bishvil she'tisasher*—Tithe in order that you become wealthy."

Our Sages are teaching that you're allowed to condition your tzedakah on Hashem's blessing. Yaakov promised to tithe properly if God would look after him properly, and we are allowed to give tzedakah and ask God to reward us with our needs and wants in return.

Which is the word common to both of these two statements of our Sages? *Bishvil*. Contextually, the word means "because" or "in order that," but the word literally means "on the path." Why is there a path between giving tzedakah and improving your life?

Rabbi Yekusiel Yehudah Teitelbaum teaches that Hashem is our Father in Heaven, and like a parent who wants to give their children everything, Hashem wants to shower us with His blessing.[2] Sometimes, all He's waiting for is a conduit through which to bring the blessing to us. That's the "path" we're creating with tzedakah. The path to sustenance that we've created for the needy person paves the way to God's provision for our needs.[3] That's why the *Rama* writes that tzedakah is the only mitzvah regarding which one may test God.[4]

However, Antignos of Socho says in *Pirkei Avos*, "Do not act as servants who attend their master merely to receive reward."[5] That complicates matters. If you're only giving tzedakah so that you'll receive a kickback, can that really be called a mitzvah?

Yes, it can. The *Divrei Yoel* explains that your soul is the purest of the pure. In truth, you *want* to do God's will. You are *passionate* about helping others. Sometimes, however, your true self doesn't shine through and reveal itself. But, Hashem figures out how to connect the dots.

---

2   *Yetev Panim.*
3   *Shov Ashiv L'Shabbos Shuvah.*
4   *Rama, Yoreh De'ah* 247:4.
5   *Avos* 1:3.

What appears to be deal-making with God is really the hand of Heaven digging deep to find and reveal the essence of your true self.[6]

Rashi approaches Antignos' dichotomy slightly differently. He teaches that the concern about making deals with Heaven is that they don't always work out. Antignos's warning is directed particularly at people who get upset at Heaven when God doesn't seem to keep His part of the deal. Antignos responds, "Stop serving God to be rewarded, and start serving Him because it's the right thing to do."

For those who are prepared to accept God's decision come what may, we may bargain and negotiate with Him. Give tzedakah with an open hand and a generosity of spirit, and Hashem will bless you with abundant prosperity.

Tithing in order to become wealthy doesn't only bring financial wealth. The Gemara expands the promise to riches throughout your life and beyond. Giving tzedakah generously engenders good health for you and your family members. Plus, it provides a special VIP section in *Olam Haba*.

The only matter that needs to be made clear before cutting any deals with God is that your faith in Him must be rock-solid. That way, you'll be able to be patient and forbearing with the Almighty and trust that He'll deliver on His part of the bargain whenever the time is right.

Always remember that our Father in Heaven knows what's best for us. Not everything we think is the best outcome is indeed the best outcome. We can make deals with the Almighty, but, ultimately, we must have faith that He knows what's best for us. May we give tzedakah generously, and may Hashem repay us with abundant prosperity, success, and good health!

---

6   *Divrei Yoel, Tazria.*

Overcoming Procrastination
(Read This Now!)

he Children of Israel were ready to leave Egypt. It had been some time since they'd been working as slaves. Over the past few months, they'd simply watched in awe as the Almighty worked wonders in the Land of Egypt. They'd gathered their belongings as well as a few souvenirs from their Egyptian neighbors. All they needed now was a departure schedule for their grand exodus.

Suddenly, Moshe announced, "Let's go!" The people were in a state of frenzy. Why so sudden? They hadn't even had enough time to prepare their bread. Couldn't they just have a day or two to get themselves and their families together?

תָּנוּ רַבָּנָן (דברים כג, כב) כִּי תִדֹּר נֶדֶר אֵין לִי אֶלָּא נֶדֶר נְדָבָה מִנַּיִן נֶאֱמַר כָּאן נֶדֶר וְנֶאֱמַר לְהַלָּן. (ויקרא ז, טז) אִם נֶדֶר אוֹ נְדָבָה מָה לְהַלָּן נְדָבָה עִמּוֹ אַף כָּאן נְדָבָה עִמּוֹ (דברים כג, כב) לַה׳ אֱלֹקֶיךָ אֵלּוּ הַדָּמִין הָעֲרָכִין וְהַחֲרָמִין וְהַהֶקְדֵּשׁוֹת (דברים כג, כב) לֹא תְאַחֵר לְשַׁלְּמוֹ הוּא וְלֹא חִלּוּפָיו.

"When you make a vow...you shall not delay paying it." From the words, "when you make a vow," I derive only the case of a vow-offering. Where do I derive the case of a gift-offering? It is stated here: "Vow," and it is stated elsewhere: "But if the sacrifice of his offering be a vow or a gift-offering." Just

11

as there a gift-offering is together with the vow, so too, here, a gift-offering is together with the vow. "To the Lord your God"—this refers to assessments, valuations, dedications, and consecrations. "You shall not delay paying it" teaches that one violates the prohibition against delaying if he is late in paying it, but not its substitute.

If you make a spiritual promise, the Torah instructs that you should not delay the fulfillment of your undertaking. Presumably, if you'd intended to do whatever it was immediately, then there'd have been no need to make an oath in the first place. Promising to do something implies a commitment to doing something at some time in the future. How long then is considered an unreasonable delay?

The Rabbis taught: Once three festivals have passed, one has transgressed, "you shall not delay." Rabbi Shimon says: three festivals in order, starting with Pesach. Rabbi Meir says: one festival. Rabbi Eliezer ben Yaakov says: two festivals. Rabbi Eliezer b'Rabbi Shimon says: Once Sukkos has passed.[1]

Certainly, the ideal way to perform a mitzvah is in the spirit of our Sages' dictum, *"Zerizim makdimim l'mitzvos*—Those who act with alacrity are the first to catch a mitzvah." Nevertheless, we're not obligated to always do everything immediately. The Torah's way to avoid procrastination is to set deadlines. The overall message of our Sages is: have a deadline. Whether it's one, two, or three festivals is debatable. But everyone agrees that some form of deadline must be set. Otherwise, the mitzvah will never be completed.

With any commitment we make in life, if we don't set a deadline, we'll never get it done. The cure for procrastination is to set solid deadlines and to stick to them. Once we've set deadlines for our tasks, we can then prioritize which tasks need to be completed first and which can be placed further down the to-do list.

---

1 *Rosh Hashanah 4b.*

Cyril N. Parkinson famously penned his law that "work expands so as to fill the time available for its completion."[2] Sometimes, I'll start writing a speech in the morning that I need to give that afternoon. It will take me all morning to prepare. Other times, I have an hour to prepare a *shiur*. Magically, my brain goes into overdrive, and I'm able to complete the preparation within the hour. Unless we set a clear and distinct deadline for a task, it will continue to weigh down upon us and impede our productivity in other areas.

Anything that's important in life must have a due date. If it's not important enough to have a due date, then it's probably not very important, and we need to ask ourselves whether it even deserves a place on our to-do list at all.

When we were about to leave Egypt, Hashem cautioned us: "You shall guard the matzos."[3] Rabbi Yoshiah expounds: Don't read it "matzos," but "mitzvos." Just like we are warned about allowing the matzos to become chametz—overstaying their time allotment—similarly, one must make sure mitzvos aren't delayed.[4] When the Almighty took us out of Egypt, He rushed us out with a clear message. If something in life is important, don't put it off. Act with alacrity and immediacy!

Rabbi Simchah Zissel Ziv teaches that the secret to avoiding procrastination is to tell yourself that today is the very last day of your life.[5] While it might sound a little depressing, it's a very motivating thought. If today's the last day, there's no pushing what's important off to tomorrow. But, still the question remains: If you have so much to accomplish today, how do you fit it all in?

The answer is scheduling. Mark out time in your diary for specific tasks. Unless you have certain times of the day to respond to emails, the entire day will be spent emailing back and forth. By the end of the day, you'll turn around and wonder what you've achieved. Most emails do not require an urgent response, and proper etiquette for general email

---

2   *Parkinson's Law: The Pursuit of Progress* (1958).

3   *Shemos* 12:17.

4   *Mechilta, Masechta D'Pischa* 9.

5   Zelig Pliskin, *Consulting the Wise*, p. 93.

and office response is twenty-four hours. You don't need to interrupt the task you're engaged in to respond to an email that has come in. If you do that, you'll never have any time to complete any significant task.

I have diarized times in my daily schedule for emails and phone-calls, for Torah study, for meetings, and for writing tasks. If I didn't set times, everything would take all-day long, and nothing substantial would be accomplished at all.

There's nothing wrong with putting things off; you simply can't do everything immediately. But, every task must have a deadline. Once you know when things need to get done by, there will be no more procrastinating. According to Rabbeinu Yonah, even the greatest sages are prone to laziness if not checked.[6] The key to overcoming laziness and the tendency to procrastinate is to allot a fixed and scheduled time for each task. May you maximize your efficiency and be extraordinarily productive and accomplished!

---

6   Rabbeinu Yonah, *Avos* 2:15, s.v. *Ha'poalim atzeilim.*

DAF 6

Respect and Openness Are Key to a Successful Marriage

The desert sun had wearied the people, and nothing Moshe did was good enough for them. The Israelites seemed to complain about almost everything. In a moment of desperation, Moshe turns his eyes Heavenward and tells the Almighty that he is not coping. "I can't carry this people on my own," he exclaims. God responds with the appointment of a cadre of seventy elders, all gifted with the Divine inspiration to prophesy.

Everyone is in awe at the power of these new prophets. They are sharing the secrets of the universe and beyond. Everyone, that is, except Moshe's wife, Tziporah. She mutters under her breath, "Well, there goes their marriages..."

Miriam hears the sigh of her sister-in-law, and she is shocked! She turns to her brother, Aharon, and cries, "We need to do something about Moshe. Why has he forsaken his wife?"

בְּךְ חֵטְא וְלֹא בְּאִשְׁתְּךָ חֵטְא סָלְקָא דַּעְתָּךְ אֲמֵינָא הוֹאִיל וְאָמַר רַבִּי יוֹחָנָן
וְאִי תֵּימָא רַבִּי אֶלְעָזָר אֵין אִשְׁתּוֹ שֶׁל אָדָם מֵתָה אֶלָּא אִם כֵּן מְבַקְשִׁין מִמֶּנּוּ
מָמוֹן וְאֵין לוֹ שֶׁנֶּאֱמַר אִם אֵין לְךָ לְשַׁלֵּם לָמָה יִקַּח מִשְׁכָּבְךָ מִתַּחְתֶּיךָ אֵימָא
בְּהַאי עָוֹן דְּבַל תְּאַחֵר נָמֵי אִשְׁתּוֹ מֵתָה קָא מַשְׁמַע לָן.

"And it would be sin in you," but there would not be a sin in your wife. It might enter your mind to suggest: Since Rabbi Yochanan, and some say Rabbi Elazar, taught: A person's wife dies only because others demand of him money and he does not have, as it is stated: "If you have nothing with which to pay, why should he take away your bed from under you?" I might suggest that one's wife also dies for the transgression of delaying the offering of a sacrifice. Therefore, the verse teaches us that this is not so.

What does the Talmud mean when it says that one's spouse dies if you do not pay back money you owe?

Prior to devoting myself full-time to the rabbinate, I worked as a financial advisor in New York City. Selling a product was a three-step process. First, there were the phone calls—sometimes referred, often cold. Once you'd established rapport with a prospective client, the second step was to have an initial meeting where you would describe a product. Step Three was to meet with them and discuss their financial portfolio in full, with the goal of closing a deal.

In setting up the final meeting, you always had to ask the question of how financial decision-making worked in their household. It would be impossible to close a deal if, at the conclusion of a pitch, the prospective client said, "Let me go home and discuss it with my spouse." In such a case, it was vital to have both spouses present so that I could discuss the matter comprehensively with both of them. Rather tellingly, however, upon my requesting that a spouse be invited to the final meeting, many prospective clients did not want their spouses present and privy to the full extent of their financial situation.

While Judaism doesn't have verbal vows, when a couple marries, the *kesubah* spells out the kind of relationship that is expected. "Be my wife according to the law of Moshe and Israel. I will work, honor, feed, and support you, as is the practice of Jewish men who work, honor, feed, and support their wives with truth."

What does the final clause mean? Is it not sufficient to work, honor, feed, and support your spouse? What is the meaning of "with truth?"

A Jewish marriage is the fusion of two halves of a soul. That doesn't happen organically because two people stood under the chuppah. It is a mission that a bride and groom commit to when they wed. Every couple is different, and each must learn how to blend his soul into one, despite his prior feelings of individualism that led him to believe that he was self-sustaining and independent. Nevertheless, certain elements are common to every marriage, which is why our Sages laid out some of the practical steps in the *kesubah* document.

One of the requirements is that every facet of the relationship is carried out "with truth." That means openness and honesty. Success in a marriage relies on sharing your every success and challenge with your spouse. And, under that category, the *kesubah* includes explicitly matters of sustenance, i.e., financial matters. Truth here means trust-worthiness and respect. Reticence to disclose the full extent of one's finances to a spouse is a mark of disrespect. It demonstrates that one believes that the other person lacks the ability to deal with such matters. That's a problem.

One of the primary causes of marital disharmony is financial stress. If you don't have an open and honest relationship with your spouse about your finances, in the words of King Solomon, "your bed will be taken from beneath you," i.e., your marriage will die. Financial struggles that you keep to yourself are liable to become an unhealthy strain on the marriage. Your spouse won't literally die, God forbid, but undoubtedly, your relationship will suffer, sometimes irreparably.

If one of the spouses believes that everything is OK and he proceeds to spend money freely while the other is stressed out about paying back the couple's debts, it's a recipe for a failed marriage. Your marriage will only be alive and real if you are completely open with your spouse. If you share your true financial situation with one another, you will be able to work together to maintain the family finances at a reasonable level and share both the challenging moments and prosperous times of life together.

The exception to this, says the Gemara, are the debts one owes to God. They're not as personally stressful because He can forgive your debts. We all have our inner spiritual struggles and challenges. Certainly, being able to share the most intimate details of your spiritual relationship with your spouse can be incredibly helpful in your spiritual growth. But, if you are not ready to do so yet, that will not ruin your marriage. Your spiritual debts impact a different marriage—your marriage with Hashem—and He is an all-understanding and forgiving spouse.

In all other matters, however, openness and honesty are the keys to a successful and long-lasting relationship. Before you got married, they may have read the traditional *tena'im,* after which the two mothers broke a plate. At that moment, the rabbi declared:

"They shall not run away nor conceal from each other anything with regard to their possessions, rather they should equally share authority over their possessions, in peace and tranquility, as is the way of those who are children of the Torah and who are in awe of God."

May you develop the trust to share your entire self with your spouse. Your marriage and life will be richer for it!

Time Waits for No Man

The Gaon of Vilna of eighteenth century Lithuania was one of the greatest Torah minds in recent history. His scholarship and diligence were both unsurpassed. His son, Avraham, once found him in tears.

"Papa, why are you crying?"

The Gaon showed his son a little notebook with times, dates, and subjects.

"You see this blank space?" the old man asked Avraham. "I was going over how I spent my time over the last twelve months, and I discovered four minutes for which I cannot account. Woe is me, they are lost forever. And now I must do *teshuvah* for those unaccounted moments!"

מֵיתִיבִי שִׁשָּׁה עָשָׂר בְּנִיסָן רֹאשׁ הַשָּׁנָה לָעוֹמֶר שִׁשָּׁה בְּסִיוָן רֹאשׁ הַשָּׁנָה לִשְׁתֵּי הַלֶּחֶם לְרָבָא לִיתְנֵי שִׁשָּׁה...רַב שִׁישָׁא בְּרֵיהּ דְּרַב אִידִי אָמַר כִּי קָא חָשֵׁיב מִידֵּי דְלָא תְּלֵי בְּמַעֲשֶׂה מִידֵּי דְּתְלֵי בְּמַעֲשֶׂה לָא קָא חָשֵׁיב.

They raised an apparent contradiction: "The sixteenth of Nissan is the New Year for the omer. The sixth of Sivan is the New Year for the two loaves. If so, according to Rava, let the Mishnah teach that there are six New Years!...Rav Shisha, son of Rav Idi explains: When the Mishnah counts New Years, it includes only those that do not depend upon an action. Those that depend upon an action (e.g., the offering of the Omer or the two loaves), it does not count.

One was not allowed to eat of the new crop until the *omer* offering was brought. Similarly, one could not bring grains as an offering in the Beis Hamikdash until the *Shtei HaLechem* were offered. Thus, these two dates effectively became the New Year for consumption of the crops, which were prohibited until those respective dates. So, if they're also considered New Years, why does our Mishnah only list four Rosh Hashanahs?

Rabbi Shisha explains that the Mishnah only includes Rosh Hashanahs that happen automatically by virtue of the date on the calendar. By contrast, these two Rosh Hashanahs don't happen unless we bring the offerings.

We're not in control of the passage of time. The Mishnah wants to warn us about the nature of a regular Rosh Hashanah; they come whether or not we are ready for them. Rosh Hashanah happens independent of human action. Even if we remain stagnant, the calendar doesn't. Life doesn't stand still. Every moment, the clock is ticking.

Here's where the Galilean principle of relativity is helpful. Imagine you are in a train traveling forward. You take a ball and throw it to your friend sitting a few seats behind you in the car. It appears to you as if the ball has traveled in the opposite direction of the train. However, someone standing outside the train with a keen eye would recognize that the ball had landed in a spot on Earth that is further toward the train's destination. You threw the ball backward, but it landed relatively forward.

Likewise, on the train of life, many of us thinking that we're just sitting in the carriage going along for the ride. And it feels like we're moving. But if you're not actually moving—in terms of growing—you only appear to be moving. Really, you haven't gone anywhere at all. In fact, relative to the train of time, you've gone backward!

The Vilna Gaon understood this well. That's why he was so distressed when he realized four minutes had passed and he couldn't recall what he had accomplished during that period of time.

Rosh Hashanah is a reminder that we are on the clock. Every minute is precious. Do you remember how you filled the last couple of hours, days, and weeks? We can't afford to just sit back and relax, because while we are relaxing, the world is moving. Every day, every hour, every minute passes, independent of what we do.

One of the traditional blessings we offer is for *"arichus yamim v'shanim,"* translated as length of days and years. What is the meaning of both long days and long years? Rav Tukachinsky explains that we are praying that one's years be many and that those years be filled with days that are well-spent and accounted for.[1]

Life happens whether or not we choose to keep up with it. Don't be left standing on the platform. May we utilize every moment to its fullest potential and experience a lifetime of extraordinary accomplishment!

---

1   *Gesher Hachaim* 3:2.

You're Not a Star — You're Even Better!

Avram Avinu has given up hope of ever becoming a father.

"Why don't you believe you will have children?" inquires the Almighty.

"For I have read it in the stars," replies the patriarch.

And so, He took him out and said to him, "Count the stars, if you can count them. Such will be your offspring!

"Leave your astrology," declares the Almighty, "I have taken you outside and above the stars. The zodiac predicted that Avram and Sarai would be childless. However, Avraham and Sarah will be the patriarch and matriarch of the Jewish People!"

כִּי חֹק לְיִשְׂרָאֵל הוּא מִשְׁפָּט לֵאלֹקֵי יַעֲקֹב תָּנוּ רַבָּנַן כִּי חֹק לְיִשְׂרָאֵל הוּא מִשְׁפָּט לֵאלֹקֵי יַעֲקֹב מְלַמֵּד שֶׁאֵין בֵּית דִּין שֶׁל מַעֲלָה נִכְנָסִין לַדִּין אֶלָּא אִם כֵּן קִידְּשׁוּ בֵּית דִּין שֶׁל מַטָה אֶת הַחֹדֶשׁ.

"For it is a law unto Israel, judgment for the God of Jacob." This teaches us that the Heavenly Court does not begin judgment until the Earthly Court has sanctified the new month.

It takes just over 29½ days for the moon to go around the earth, so every Jewish month, toward which only complete days can be counted, ends up consisting of either 29 or 30 days. In Temple times, witnesses would come to the High Court in Jerusalem and testify as to when they had spotted the new moon. Once validated, the Court would declare that the new month had arrived.

The Gemara notes that, since the new month is not in effect until the Court has said so, Rosh Hashanah, which falls on the first of the month, cannot happen until the Court decides. And since Rosh Hashanah is the day when Hashem judges the world, He cannot begin judgment in the Heavenly Court until the Earthly Court has declared the day as Rosh Hashanah!

Rabbi Yekusiel Yehudah Teitelbaum comments that we have a relationship of reciprocity with the Almighty.[1] He will not judge us until we have informed Him that it is time for us to be judged by Him. When He receives our signal, He places us directly under the jurisdiction of His providence. We could choose not to submit ourselves to His dominion. What would then happen is that we would fall under the dominion of the forces of nature.

God's message to Avram was that by entering into the covenant with Him, he was placing himself above the forces of nature. No longer would the stars have any power over him. God alone would determine his fate and destiny. By our religious actions, we rise above the stars, and we overcome any predestined natural course. *Mazal* plays a role, but Torah and mitzvos play an even greater role. In fact, the mitzvah of sanctifying the new month of Tishrei demonstrates that even the Almighty Himself, so to speak, is directed by the power of our mitzvah performance.

The Kotzker Rebbe once turned to his *chassidim* and asked, "Where is God?"

"He is everywhere," they responded in unison.

"No," replied the Kotzker, "God is wherever you let Him in."

The Talmud is teaching us that we have the power to invite Hashem into our world. Until we declare that we are renewed and sanctified, the Almighty does not enter. You get to choose whether to invite God into your life or to be directed by the forces of nature. Invite Him into your world! Let Him guide you through life. Your life will be out of this world.

---

1   *Yetev Panim*, Pesach.

If We're Servants of Hashem, Are We Truly Free?

There's a famine in Canaan. Yitzchak decides to follow in the footsteps of his parents. He takes Rivkah, and off they travel to Gerar. Like Avraham and Sarah, they pretend to be brother and sister. But this time, King Avimelech does not fall for the ruse. He keeps an ever-watchful eye over their behavior and soon spots them behaving like a married couple. After a brief altercation, Avimelech showers Yitzchak and Rivkah with gifts and implores his people to treat them with respect.

As Yitzchak begins to lay down his roots and build his business in Gerar, however, the locals begin to get jealous of his success. Every time he digs a well and finds water, his competitors claim the well as their own. Eventually, he is forced to leave Gerar and heads back off to Canaan.

אָמַר קְרָא וּקְרָאתֶם דְּרוֹר בָּאָרֶץ...דְּתַנְיָא אֵין דְּרוֹר אֶלָּא לְשׁוֹן חֵירוּת אָמַר רַבִּי יְהוּדָה מָה לְשׁוֹן דְּרוֹר כִּמְדַיֵּיר בֵּי דַיָּירָא וּמוֹבִיל סְחוֹרָה בְּכָל מְדִינָה.

The verse states: "And you shall proclaim liberty [dror] in the land." As it is taught: The word dror is a term meaning "liberty." Rabbi Yehudah said: What is the meaning of the word dror? It is like a man who dwells [medayer] in any dwelling-place and can move his merchandise through every country.

In the jubilee year, we proclaim liberty for all. Rabbi Yehudah explains the etymology of the word for liberty. It comes from the word meaning "to dwell," since a free man can "dwell in any dwelling-place and move his merchandise through every country." Why does Rabbi Yehudah add the idea of moving merchandise? It seems to have nothing to do with the word *dror*, which refers to the first part of his explanation that he may "dwell in any place."

Rabbi Yehudah is teaching us that, although "liberty has been proclaimed in the land," we are not truly free until we can expand our freedoms to every place and every country. Freedom should be for all peoples in all places. As Jews, we appreciate the constraints on freedom that many regimes impose on their inhabitants. For most of our history, even those countries that allowed us to stay often maintained restrictions on our entry into professional life, land ownership, and even the free practice of our religion. Given our personal experience, we are equipped with the understanding and responsibility to defend the freedoms of all peoples from tyranny and persecution.

Over the centuries, one of the areas in which we've become particularly strong is cross-border trade. Since we were denied land ownership, we had to master commercial activities that were not tied to real estate and were not location-specific. This free-trade idea is fundamental to Rabbi Yehudah's conception of freedom.

Nevertheless, at the end of the day, even nomads need green pastures and fresh water for their flocks, and that's what Yitzchak struggled with. He required natural land-based resources to sustain his commercial enterprise. All the gifts of Avimelech were wonderful, but he needed to anchor them in real property.

That's the blessing of the Promised Land. As long as Yitzchak was in Gerar, he was at the mercy of the Philistines who claimed the land and natural resources as their own. That's been the attitude of many nations of the world throughout our exile. They became jealous anytime we were successful, accusing us of taking advantage of their resources. In the thirteenth and fourteenth centuries, for example, the Jewish communities of France and England felt like tennis balls as they were continuously expelled and readmitted between the two countries.

The only guarantee of our safety and security is the Promised Land. No matter how prosperous we become in exile, we have a fundamental need for Israel, our homeland.

What, then, is the freedom of which Rabbi Yehudah speaks? Isn't the ultimate freedom the ability to have no ties and be able to live anywhere?

That's what we thought initially when we left the slavery of Egypt. Finally, we were free. We had no responsibilities. There was nothing to tie us down. No sooner had we left Egypt, however, and the Almighty showed us the true meaning of freedom. Liberty requires an anchor in some form of emotional sustenance, meaning, and direction. God offered it to us with the giving of the Torah.

Unlike Egypt, where we were slaves, the Torah itself makes it clear that we have the freedom to choose to accept or reject His Torah and mitzvos, as it states, "Behold, I have placed before you today life and good, and death and bad."[1] The *Ramban* comments that we have two paths from which to choose, and the permission is ours to take whichever path we desire, with no impediment from above or below. Similarly, the *Rambam* writes, "Every person has the right to pick the good direction and become righteous, or to pick the bad direction and become wicked."[2]

Liberty allows us to be whoever we like, wherever we like, but the wise individual will appreciate that, without an anchor, freedom becomes meaningless.

Most of us today are blessed to be living in countries that share our value of freedom. May we merit to see the day when we will be able to "proclaim liberty" for all peoples of the world. May you never take your liberty for granted and exercise your right to anchor yourself in the ways of Hashem.

---

1   *Devarim* 30:15.
2   *Rambam, Mishneh Torah, Teshuvah*, chap. 5.

Become an Ambassador of Heaven!

abbi Yehuda HaNasi, known as Rebbi, would often meet with his friend, the Roman Emperor, Antoninus. The Emperor would consult with Rebbi on a range of issues, ranging from the personal to the political. For example, prior to embarking on his military expedition to Egypt, he discussed the matter with Rebbi, who encouraged his efforts, drawing inspiration from the prophecies of Yechezkel.

Even when his personal and political worlds collided, Rebbi was there for him to help him view the situation objectively and impartially. On one such occasion, Antoninus arrived at his meeting with Rebbi, faced with a conundrum. He had the opportunity to make one special request of the Roman Senate. He was torn between two choices. Should he use the opportunity to request that his son be appointed as his successor? Or should he utilize the moment to elevate Tiberius's status to that of a colony? The former was, undoubtedly, tainted by his personal bias; the latter was an important political move. And yet, he couldn't bring his head to overrule his heart. He turned to Rebbi, hoping for some sage advice.

Rebbi responded, "Appoint your son as your successor. Once he succeeds you, he can take steps to elevate the status of Tiberius."[1]

תַּנְיָא רַבִּי אֱלִיעֶזֶר אוֹמֵר בְּתִשְׁרֵי נִבְרָא הָעוֹלָם רַבִּי יְהוֹשֻׁעַ אוֹמֵר בְּנִיסָן נִבְרָא הָעוֹלָם.

Rabbi Eliezer says the world was created in the month of Tishrei, Rabbi Yehoshua says the world was created in Nissan.

Which one was it? Was the world created in Tishrei or Nissan? The dichotomy appears to play out in our Jewish calendars. We celebrate Rosh Hashanah at the beginning of Tishrei. But, at the same time, the Torah calls Tishrei "the seventh month." How are we to make sense of this apparent contradiction?

The Arizal likens the process to the two stages of conception and birth, the former taking place at Tishrei and the latter at Nissan.[2] Hence, the prayer we recite following the shofar blasts on Rosh Hashanah is, "Today is the conception of the world." Practically speaking, what is the difference between the two stages of the spiritual conception and birth of the world?

According to Rabbi Levi Yitzchak of Berditchev, although the world was created in Tishrei, nevertheless, in Nissan the purpose of the world was revealed, which sealed the deal on creation.[3] The primary purpose of creation is that we should perform God's will and publicize His greatness. Not until the miracles and wonders of the Exodus and the birth of the Israelite nation did this purpose become clear to the world.

In this vein, Rabbi Jonathan Sacks compares and contrasts the two annual festival cycles. Tishrei consists of Rosh Hashanah, Yom Kippur, and Sukkos. Nissan begins the cycle of the pilgrimage festivals: Pesach, Shavuos, and Sukkos. The former set symbolizes Hashem's role as Creator, whereas the second represent His role as Redeemer. Creation is a universalistic experience, common to the entire world. Redemption was a particularistic experience, unique to the Jewish People.

---

1   *Avodah Zarah* 10a.
2   *Pri Eitz Chaim*, cited in *Ohr HaMeir*, Pesach.
3   *Kedushas Levi, Derush l'Pesach.*

Sukkos, explains Rabbi Sacks, contains both elements of universalism and particularism, and therefore it appears in both sets. On the one hand, we pray for all nations, offering seventy sacrifices through the course of the holiday. We also shake the lulav and esrog, which impacts the weather and climate for the year ahead,[4] a further manifestation of Sukkos's status as a festival with a universalistic dimension. On the other hand, we dwell in the sukkah to acknowledge the Almighty's protection of His covenantal people—first amidst the sojourn through the wilderness and then throughout millennia of exile.[5]

These two aspects—the universal and the particular—are paramount to our understanding of ourselves and our purpose in the world. We were created by the Almighty to make this world a better place. We have a duty to be citizens of the world and be an ambassador of the Almighty. When the world sees the positive role played by the Jewish People, it is a tribute to our Creator. Just like Rebbi, we must find ways to shine and make an impact, not just upon the Jewish community, but upon larger society.

So, which one was it, Tishrei or Nissan? Rabbeinu Bachya teaches that the Torah lands on Tishrei. The first word בראשית contains many secrets, one of which is the date: א' בתשרי.[6]

Both are integral. A strong Jewish commitment and identity is an essential prerequisite for the universal contribution that you will make. May you be a shining *kiddush Hashem* for the Jewish community and far beyond.

---

4   *Taanis* 2b.
5   Rabbi Jonathan Sacks, *Ceremony & Celebration* (2017), p. 109.
6   *Bereishis* 1:2.

You Are Not Mediocre!

Akiva was a dedicated shepherd to his flock. Skillful and diligent, shepherding came naturally to him. The truth is that it hadn't ever really occurred to him to do anything different. Shepherding was what he knew, and shepherding was what he was good at. He would wake up early to tend the sheep and put in a good day's work. By the time he sat down each evening, all he could think about was his head hitting the pillow.

But his wife, Rachel, wasn't satisfied with his attitude to life. "Why don't you spend a half hour each day learning a little Torah?" she would ask.

"Look," he would reply, "I'm just a simple shepherd. My head was not manufactured for Torah learning."

But then, one day, he chanced upon a rock. This rock was unlike any other he'd ever seen. The middle of the rock had hollowed out. Just above, there was water seeping out of the cliff-face, drop by drop. It seems that over many years, the droplets had managed to bore a hole in the rock.

Akiva looked at the rock in wonder and exclaimed, "If water can make a hole in a solid rock, then surely Torah can make its way into my unlearned head!" He decided then and there to take some time off to dedicate himself to Torah study. By the time he returned from his studies, Rabbi Akiva was one of the greatest Torah Sages ever to walk the face of the Earth.

בְּרֹאשׁ הַשָּׁנָה בָּטְלָה עֲבוֹדָה מֵאֲבוֹתֵינוּ בְּמִצְרָיִם. תּוֹס': וְאע"פ שהתחילו המכות מניסן דמשפט המצרים י"ב חדש כדתנן בעדיות מ"מ לא פסקה עבודה עד תשרי.

On Rosh Hashanah, the slavery of our ancestors in Egypt ceased. Tosafos: The plagues began in Nissan, for the judgment of the Egyptians endured twelve months. Nevertheless, the slavery did not end until Tishrei.

If the slavery ended in Tishrei, *Tosafos* points out that during the first five plagues, the Children of Israel were still enslaved. Picture it: The Egyptians were looking far and wide for pure water to drink because everything had turned to blood. Their lives had been completely disrupted because there were frogs everywhere. They couldn't stop scratching themselves because the land was writhing with lice. There were wild animals everywhere wreaking havoc, and then all the beasts died, spreading physical contamination.

And while all this was going on, the Israelites just kept showing up to work, day in and day out. They just continued doing their thing: looking for straw, making bricks, building pyramids—oblivious to the chaos around them.

Until one day, somebody woke up and thought to himself, "You know, we probably don't have to do this anymore. If I don't show up to work today, who's going to report me?" And he stayed home. And nothing happened. Slowly but surely, his bold idea spread, and eventually all the Jews realized that the slavery was a thing of the past.

But why did it take them six months to figure that out?

Sometimes we're so used to doing what we do that we get stuck in a rut. Our poor ancestors had been slaves for two hundred and ten years. That's all they knew. Any other life didn't ever occur to them. The only life they were familiar with was the one where you get up each day and work as a slave to Pharaoh. It was a massive paradigm shift to begin to imagine that life could be any different.

That was Rabbi Akiva's problem too. He was a shepherd because he'd been born into a family of shepherds, and that was all he'd ever imagined doing with his life. That's not to say there's anything wrong with being a shepherd. If one acts in a dignified and proper manner, any profession may be the right profession for an individual. The problem occurs when we're passively engaged in an occupation, simply by virtue of having gone with the flow, never having given much thought to our choices in life.

Rabbi Akiva was scared to dream big. He couldn't imagine becoming a Rabbinic superstar. But Rachel, his pious wife, knew what great potential he had. She was able to snap him out of his mediocrity, and with a little help from nature, Akiva was able to transform his way of thinking. Once he shifted his ways of thinking, he could achieve anything.

We're all familiar with the classic story of the *balabusta* who would always cut off the ends of her roast before cooking it. Upon being questioned as to this strange practice, she explains that she was taught to prepare it that way by her mother. They call the mother and ask her for an explanation and she says that she was taught to do it that way by her mother.

One visit later to the seniors' home and everything becomes clear.

"Why would I always cut off the ends of my roast before cooking it?" chuckles the old lady, "Well, back in the day, we couldn't afford a large pot. So, I had to cut off the ends to fit the piece of meat into the small pot."

While people often quote this fable to criticize the abundance of meaningless customs and rituals, in actuality, it is a sad reflection of most people's day-to-day lives. So many things that we do, so many ways we act, we do so without giving it much thought and intent. We just do things the way that we've always done them, never asking ourselves whether we could be acting in a more effective, accomplished manner.

It's time to stop and think. Why do we behave the way we do? Are we achieving the very best in life that we have the potential to be? Have we taken ownership of our spiritual life? Or are we living a life bequeathed to us that we've never really contemplated?

It's time to wake up and take life by the reins. Stop working for Pharaoh; he's not even watching! We have unlimited potential. When we dream big, you can accomplish amazing things in life.

It's time you figured out for yourself the most spiritually enriching way to lead your life and the goals that you can achieve in every aspect of your life. May the Almighty bestow you with the wisdom to seek, find, and own your true, extraordinary self. Your life will become eternally meaningful and blessed.

Don't Bottle Up Your Anger!

Yosef's brothers were jealous of him. How much more of his silly dream-talk could they take? To make matters worse, despite the nonsense he spoke, their father appeared to love Yosef more and more! It wasn't about the colorful coat; that's not what bothered them.

Actually, they couldn't really put their finger on what disturbed them so much. Was it the extra care and attention their father was giving him? Not really. That was understandable, given Yaakov's love for Rachel. Why did they despise their brother?

Their feelings of anger and jealousy were burning up inside of them. Each day, the animosity grew stronger and stronger. Meanwhile, Yosef was oblivious to their derision. So, when Yaakov asked Yosef to take provisions over to his brothers as they were shepherding in the field, he jumped to his feet, ready for the mission. After all, he craved nothing more than his brothers' recognition and acceptance.

אָמַר רַב חִסְדָּא בְּרוֹתְחִין קִלְקְלוּ וּבְרוֹתְחִין נִידּוֹנוּ בְּרוֹתְחִין קִלְקְלוּ בַּעֲבֵירָה וּבְרוֹתְחִין נִידּוֹנוּ כְּתִיב הָכָא וַיִּשֹׁכּוּ הַמַּיִם וּכְתִיב הָתָם וַחֲמַת הַמֶּלֶךְ שָׁכָכָה. רש"י: וחמת המלך שככה—וסתם חמה חמה רותחת היא כדכתיב וחמתו בערה בו.

Rav Chisda taught: The generation of the Great Flood sinned with boiling hot passion, and they were punished with boiling hot water; they sinned with the boiling passion of sin, and they were punished with boiling hot water. It is written here, "And the waters abated," and it is written there (in the Megillah), "And the heated anger of the king abated" [which implies that the word "abated" means cooled and implies that at first the waters of the flood had been boiling hot]. Rashi: Typical anger is boiling, as it says, "And his anger was burning inside."

Rashi's description of "typical anger" implies that there is also a kind of anger that is not typical. If typical anger boils, then the other kind of anger doesn't boil; it just simmers.

The Torah instructs, "Do not despise your brother in your heart, you shall surely *communicate* with your fellow, and not carry iniquity on his account."[1]

Traditionally, these words being translated as "communicate with your fellow" have been translated as "rebuke your fellow." Rebuke is rarely effective. It might work in the short-term. Over the long-term, however, it tends to lead to resentment and even greater ill-feeling between people. In fact, our Sages teach that nowadays, nobody knows how to rebuke anymore [2]—and that was in Talmudic times. Certainly, in our time, pure chastisement is probably not the answer. The reason for our inability to rebuke is that we are rarely able to sift out our own feelings and emotions from those words of condemnation. Consequently, it's not truly a pure critique that's being offered and, therefore, it won't achieve the desired results.

A more useful approach is to think of the Torah's instruction in terms of "communication." When you have an issue with someone, don't let the upset simmer inside of you. You need to sit them down and communicate with them directly. Otherwise, you will carry sin on that person's account. What that means is that you will be filled with unhappiness about the relationship, while the other person is proceeding along on his merry way, completely oblivious to the issue. While you're burning up—or simmering—inside, he's content and not bothered in the

---

1   *Vayikra* 19:17.
2   *Arachin* 16b.

slightest. You may feel that he's acted inappropriately toward you, but unless you're prepared to discuss the matter with him, you and you alone will carry the burden of the "iniquity."

When I offer premarital counseling to young couples, one of the commitments I ask them to make to one another is that they will seek counseling should the relationship ever go awry. Sadly, too many marriages break up with one of the partners deciding that he's had enough and simply walking out. Meanwhile, the other partner is sitting there in shock, having never realized that her spouse was so unhappy. Had the spouse sought help, the marriage very often could have been saved. But by the time it's over, it's often way too late for that.

That's what was happening between Yosef and his brothers. They were burning up inside, while he was oblivious to their discontent. Had they simply been prepared to sit down and have a mature conversation, we might have been saved all the grief of the exile and slavery in Egypt. But they just couldn't bring themselves to talk about their issues.

Although our Sages teach: "On account of two *selas* weight of fine wool that Yaakov gave Yosef over his other sons, his brothers became jealous of him, and the matter evolved and our forefathers descended to Egypt,"[3] it's clear from the Torah's account that their jealousy went way beyond a piece of clothing. Jealousy implies resentment and is not necessarily tied to any one particular thing. It means despising someone simply because he is in a position that irks you. You might not even desire to be in his place. You're just simmering with resentment in your heart about his good fortune. What then happens is that the feelings of resentment start to overpower you so that every little thing the other person does bothers you. You can't really put your finger on the problem. You just can't stand that person.

Maintaining your anger at a simmering point is dangerous. You need to talk about issues that are bothering you before the anger boils over. That means asserting yourself and discussing your problems with your spouse or others in your life with whom you're struggling. Maybe

---

3   *Shabbos* 10b.

what's holding you back is the concern that you'll lose your cool and present yourself inappropriately. But it's much better that you get it out of your system now, rather than explode later when the relationship is beyond repair.

If you have simmering anger issues, the key is to get them off your chest as soon as you can. Holding them in will only make matters worse in the long run. Talk to your spouse or friend or colleague. If you need to, seek counsel from a third party. Sometimes, it helps just to have someone else at the table. And, more often than not, a professional third-party can be particularly helpful; it's probably not the first time that the person has encountered whatever issues you have.

Don't let that anger simmer. You're only making yourself miserable by carrying the iniquity. And in the long run, everyone will suffer. May we master the art of communication and maintain healthy and clear relationships!

Belief in the Rabbis

A conversion candidate once appeared before the great sage, Shammai. He said to Shammai, "How many Torahs do you have?" Shammai replied, "We have two, the Written Torah and the Oral Torah."

The fellow said to him, "With regard to the Written Torah, I believe you, but with regard to the Oral Torah, I do not believe you. Convert me on condition that you will teach me only the Written Torah." Shammai refused his ridiculous demand in no uncertain terms.

He then appeared before Hillel, who agreed to convert him and began teaching him Torah. On the first day, he showed him the letters of the *aleph-beis* and said to him: *Aleph, beis, gimmel, dalet*. The next day he reversed the order of the letters.

Bewildered, the convert said to him, "But yesterday you did not tell me that! It was the other way around!"

Hillel replied, "Didn't you rely on my authority as to the order of the letters? Therefore, it only makes sense to rely on me, as well, with regard to the matter of the Oral Torah, and accept the interpretations that I teach you."[1]

וְקִים לְהוּ לְרַבָּנַן דְּכָל תְּבוּאָה שֶׁנִּקְצְרָה בֶּחָג בְּיָדוּעַ שֶׁהֵבִיאָה שְׁלִישׁ לִפְנֵי רֹאשׁ הַשָּׁנָה וְקָא קָרֵי לַהּ בְּצֵאת הַשָּׁנָה אָמַר לֵיהּ רַבִּי יִרְמְיָה לְרַבִּי זֵירָא וְקִים לְהוּ

---

1   *Shabbos* 31a.

לְרַבָּנָן בֵּין שְׁלִישׁ לִפְחוֹת מִשְּׁלִישׁ אֲמַר לֵיהּ לָאו אָמֵינָא לָךְ לָא תִּפֵּיק נַפְשָׁךְ
לְבַר מֵהִלְכְתָא כָּל מִדּוֹת חֲכָמִים כֵּן הוּא אַרְבָּעִים סְאָה הוּא טוֹבֵל בְּאַרְבָּעִים
סְאָה חָסֵר קוֹרְטוֹב אֵינוֹ יָכוֹל לִטְבּוֹל בָּהֶן כְּבֵיצָה מְטַמֵּא טוּמְאַת אוֹכְלִין
כְּבֵיצָה חָסֵר שׁוּמְשׁוּם אֵינוֹ מְטַמֵּא טוּמְאַת אוֹכְלִין שְׁלֹשָׁה עַל שְׁלֹשָׁה מְטַמֵּא
מִדְרָס שְׁלֹשָׁה עַל שְׁלֹשָׁה חָסֵר נִימָא אַחַת אֵינוֹ מְטַמֵּא מִדְרָס הֲדַר אֲמַר רַבִּי
יִרְמְיָה לָאו מִילְּתָא הִיא דַּאֲמָרִי.

The Sages have a tradition that any grain that is harvested on Sukkos is known to have reached one-third of its growth before Rosh Hashanah, and the Torah calls that period of the year "at the end of the year." Rabbi Yirmiyah said to Rabbi Zeira: "And are the Sages able to discern precisely between produce that reached one-third of its growth and produce that reached less than one-third of its growth?" Rabbi Zeira said to him: "Do I not always tell you that you must not take yourself out of the bounds of the halachah? All the measures of the Sages are like this; they are precise and exact. For example, one who immerses himself in a mikvah containing forty se'ah of water is rendered pure, but in forty se'ah minus the tiny amount of a kortov, he cannot immerse and become pure in them. Similarly, an egg-bulk of impure food can render other food ritually impure, but an egg-bulk minus even the tiny amount of a sesame seed does not render food ritually impure. So too, a piece of cloth three-by-three handbreadths in size is susceptible to ritual impurity imparted by treading, but a piece of cloth three-by-three handbreadths minus one hair is not susceptible to ritual impurity imparted by treading." Rabbi Yirmiyah then said: "What I said is nothing."

When Moshe stood atop Mt. Sinai, he received both a Written Torah and an Oral Torah. The latter is the explanation of the former. Without it, it is impossible to discern the true meaning of the text. Even before one wishes to ascertain meaning beyond the text, one must be able to read the text, which appears with neither vowels nor punctuation. Only with the assistance of the Oral Torah can one read the words and sentences. And only with the guidance of our Sages are we able to appreciate the true meaning of the text. The teachings of Chazal form an essential element of the Oral Law.

For example, the word for "milk" in Hebrew is "*chalav.*" The same word could also be read "*chelev,*" which means "fats." Without the guidance of the Oral tradition, we might have thought that we could not mix meat and meat-fats. Only when we read the Divine text with the direction of our Sages' explanations do we know God's intent.

Throughout our history, movements questioning the veracity of the Oral Torah have arisen, from the Sadducees to the Karaites, and many others. Adherents of these groups did not practice Judaism homogeneously, as each felt that their understanding of the meaning of Scripture was the most precise. By contrast, traditional Judaism has maintained a consistency and uniformity across the globe and across history, such that the differences in religious observance between traditional Jews are so minor that they have never constituted a fissure in the tradition. A Sephardic Jew can pray in an Ashkenazic shul and eat in a Yemenite home, with the knowledge and comfort that the prayer service and the food will meet a familiar and acceptable religious standard.

What's the secret to the maintenance of the homogeneity of traditional Jewish practice and belief? Our fealty to the precision and integrity of our Sages. *Emunas Chachamim*—belief in the words of our Rabbis, is integral to our tradition. If we were to start questioning the accuracy of our Sages in one area, the entire foundation of Judaism would collapse.

The first person to question the Oral Law was Korach. He rallied the troops against Moshe's authority with arguments that sounded halachically reasonable.

"If you had a room full of Torah scrolls, why would you need a mezuzah on the doorpost?"

"If you were wearing a garment completely colored with *techeles*, blue dye, why would it still require *techeles* on the fringes?"

These contentions might sound reasonable, but if every point were arguable, then Torah would lack all foundation. The *Rambam* explains that there are certain fundamentals that Moshe received at Mt. Sinai that are not debatable.[2] *Machlokes*—halachic debate, exists within certain well-defined parameters. There is an agreed-upon set of laws and principles that one must accept in order to participate. That starting point is that Chazal have a received tradition from Sinai and that their system of interpretation and exposition is precise and accurate.

For example, says the *Rambam*, when the Torah states that one must take the "fruit of a beautiful tree" as one of the four species on Sukkos,[3] we do not find a single sage throughout the period from Moshe until the Gemara who suggested this commandment referred to anything but an esrog. Debates may exist concerning the kashrus of an esrog that contained a particular mark on its skin, but all agree that the mitzvah may only be performed with a certain species of fruit and that it must be taken in conjunction with three other agreed-upon species.

The Torah declares, "According to the Torah they shall teach you, and the judgment they shall tell you, you shall do. You shall not deviate from the word they tell you right or left."[4]

Rashi comments that the Torah is instructing us that we would be required to adhere to the guidance of our Sages, even if they were to tell us that "right is left and left is right. How much more so, given the fact that they tell us that right is right and left is left!"[5] The *Sifsei Chachamim* explains that the Almighty infuses His spirit into the words of the Sages and guards them from error, ensuring the truth of their rulings and teachings.

Indeed, axiomatically, the rulings of the Sages are true. Once the Torah has invested them with the authority to determine the law, their utterances are, by definition, accurate. Provided a *posek* is fit to render a halachic ruling and has taken all necessary steps to peruse and understand the minutiae of the particular issue, his ruling becomes definitive halachah, even if his decision does not align with Heaven's perspective.[6]

---

2   Intro to Mishnah 4 (*Rambam La'Am*, p. 30).
3   *Vayikra* 23:40.
4   *Devarim* 17:11.
5   Based on *Sifri* 154.
6   *Igros Moshe*, intro para. 2.

An excellent example is the famous story of the Achnai oven. When Rabbi Eliezer disagreed with the consensus position, he called upon a higher power for support. A Heavenly voice issued forth and backed his ruling. Nevertheless, Rabbi Yehoshua wouldn't budge. The law was already determined by the Torah, when it declared that the majority Rabbinic rule would determine halachah. Thus, by definition, the halachah accorded with the consensus opinion, regardless of any Divine support offered in favor of Rabbi Eliezer's opinion.

Essential to our religious faith is the belief in the teachings of our Sages. Even when they don't appear to make sense, we must adopt the attitude of our ancestors, *"naaseh v'nishma"*—we will perform our religious duties, with the pure and faithful acceptance of the yoke of our heritage. That declaration we made regarding both the Written Law and the Oral Law, and the teachings of Chazal are part and parcel of the Oral Law.

The exchange between Rabbi Yirmiyah and Rabbi Zeira in our Gemara demonstrates that even the most learned rabbis can harbor doubts and misgivings about our *mesorah*. Sometimes, the struggle with one's faith is even greater when the doubts surround the teachings of the Sages. But we are *maaminim b'nei maaminim*. Upon leaving Egypt, we committed to *emunas Chachamim*, as the Torah attests, "and they believed in Hashem and in Moshe His servant."[7] May you always maintain faith in the Torah and its teachers!

---

7   *Shemos* 15:31.

Why Bother with Chumros?

R abbi Chanina ben Teradyon was one of the great Torah teachers, who was persecuted, and ultimately martyred, at the hands of the Romans for teaching Torah. He was once asked about his place in Heaven. He responded that he was quite sure that he had a share in the World to Come on account of a charitable deed that he had performed once. He was on the way to purchase food for his Purim feast when he encountered some poor people. He immediately disbursed the funds. He then made up his mind that he would not recoup the funds from his charitable donations fund, as he wanted the mitzvah to be pure and selfless.

Rabbi Chanina's interlocutor pressed him, "Surely, *rebbi*, you must have a share in *Olam Haba* based on your extraordinary dedication to teaching Torah publicly!"

Rabbi Chanina replied, "Teaching Torah is a big mitzvah. But it's a mitzvah, I'm afraid, that is tainted by the honor that I am accorded by my brethren, who treat me as a famous and illustrious sage. That act of tzedakah came with no personal benefit or gain. That mitzvah will guarantee my place in the World to Come."[1]

תַּנְיָא לְעוֹלָם הֲלָכָה כְּדִבְרֵי בֵּית הִלֵּל וְהָרוֹצֶה לַעֲשׂוֹת כְּדִבְרֵי בֵּית שַׁמַּאי עוֹשֶׂה כְּדִבְרֵי בֵּית הִלֵּל עוֹשֶׂה מִקּוּלֵי בֵּית שַׁמַּאי וּמִקּוּלֵי בֵּית הִלֵּל רָשָׁע

---

1   *Avodah Zarah* 18a.

מֵחוּמְרֵי בֵית שַׁמַּאי וּמֵחוּמְרֵי בֵית הִלֵּל עָלָיו הַכָּתוּב אוֹמֵר וְהַכְּסִיל בַּחֹשֶׁךְ הוֹלֵךְ אֶלָּא אִי כְּבֵית שַׁמַּאי בְּקוּלֵּיהוֹן וּבְחוּמְרֵיהוֹן אִי כְּבֵית הִלֵּל בְּקוּלֵּיהוֹן וּבְחוּמְרֵיהוֹן.

רש"י: מִקּוּלֵי ב"ש כו'—אֲבָל בב' מַחְלוֹקוֹת שֶׁהִקֵּילוּ אֵלּוּ בְּזוֹ וְאֵלּוּ בְּזוֹ אֵין כָּאן לֹא מִשּׁוּם רָשָׁע וְלֹא מִשּׁוּם סִכְלוּת דִּסְבִירָא לֵיהּ בְּהָא כב"ש וּבְהָא כְּבֵית הִלֵּל.

The halachah is always in accordance with the statement of Beis Hillel, but one who wishes to act in accordance with the statement of Beis Shammai may do so, and one who wishes to act in accordance with the statement of Beis Hillel may do so. One who adopts both the leniencies of Beis Shammai and the leniencies of Beis Hillel is wicked. And if he adopts both the stringencies of Beis Shammai and the stringencies of Beis Hillel, with regard to him the verse states: "The fool walks in darkness." Rather, one should act either in accordance with Beis Shammai, following both their leniencies and their stringencies, or in accordance with Beis Hillel, following both their leniencies and their stringencies.

Rashi: Concerning two separate debates, however, where one opinion is more lenient in one instance, but the other is more lenient in the other case, this would not constitute wickedness or foolishness. Rather, he holds like Beis Shammai in one case and like Beis Hillel in the other.

Some people love "rabbi-shopping." Rabbi-shopping is the phenomenon where one seeks to always find the rabbi with the most lenient opinion in every matter of Jewish law. There are rabbis who will allow you to *kasher* kitchen items for Pesach that others wouldn't. There are rabbis who are known for their *heterim* in the area of *taharas ha'mishpachah*. If you ask around, it's not too difficult to find a rabbi in good standing who has permitted certain practices, despite holding a minority view compared to his colleagues. The art of rabbi-shopping is mastering the ability to find the rabbi who is most lenient in each particular situation.

Rashi explains that the concern with following the leniencies of both Beis Hillel and Beis Shammai or the stringencies of both only applies when maintaining both positions would be contradictory. One may, however, adopt multiple leniencies or multiple stringencies from different rabbis in entirely unconnected areas of halachah. And so, *Rashi* would permit rabbi-shopping "where one agrees with the rationale of one rabbi in one case and another rabbi in a different case."

What *Rashi* is emphasizing is that you shouldn't go rabbi-shopping just because you are looking for the easy way out. If you sincerely agree with one rabbi in a particular situation and a different rabbi in a completely different scenario, that's acceptable. A litmus test to determine whether you are acting sincerely is to ask yourself how often you adopt the stringent position. If you never adopt stringencies, then you are obviously just looking for the easy way out and justifying the rationale in each case accordingly.

Stringencies—*chumros*, aren't just for fools. If a rabbi has ruled stringently on a case, he's not just doing so to push his weight around and make your life difficult. He's doing it because he believes that's what God wants.

"Rabbi Chananiah ben Akashia says: The Holy One, blessed be He, wanted to give merit to Israel. Therefore, he gave them an abundance of Torah and mitzvos."[2] Why would an abundance of mitzvos give us merit? Wouldn't it just increase our load and make it ever more difficult to fulfill the will of Heaven?

It comes down to perspective. If you view mitzvos as a burden, then indeed, any additional mitzvos are cause for greater concern and resentment. If, however, you understand that mitzvos are a way to connect with our Father in Heaven, then each mitzvah is an *opportunity* to strengthen the Divine bond.

Our relationship with Hashem is like a marriage. You could feel resentful about making dinner for your spouse, or you could see even the most mundane household "chores" as opportunities to demonstrate

---

2   *Makkos* 16:3.

your love for your partner. Every time you take out the garbage is another chance to strengthen the bonds of marriage. Saying "I love you" is beautiful, but actions speak much louder.

In the same way, prayer is an excellent way to connect with Hashem, but mitzvah performance is far more powerful. That's why Hashem gave us an abundance of mitzvos. Graciously, He wanted to afford us limitless opportunities to connect with Him.

When you understand mitzvos as opportunities, you don't seek to run away from *chumros*. Wouldn't you want to connect with Hashem in the deepest way possible? What's more, given the power the Torah invests in the words of our Sages, a bona fide *chumrah* takes the force of the mitzvah and affords us yet another opportunity to deepen our relationship with Hashem. That's not something to avoid; we should be seeking to maximize those opportunities!

The *Rambam* has a slightly different take on the Mishnah. He explains that in order to enter *Olam Haba*, one must fulfill one mitzvah with utter sincerity and purity. Hashem provided us with an abundance of mitzvos, most of which we will fulfill driven by ulterior motives such as peer and social pressures. But amongst the multitude of mitzvos, un-doubtedly, we will all find one mitzvah that we can perform completely undiluted by any external factors. For Rabbi Chanina ben Teradion, explains the *Rambam*, that mitzvah was the charity he gave from his Purim meal funds.

Chumros aren't easy to take on, but that extra effort increases the chances that we will fulfill the mitzvah with wholehearted sincerity. The most important thing that the Almighty wants from you is that no matter what position you choose to take, you do not disparage anyone else for choosing a more lenient or stricter position. If there is a valid Torah opinion that has ruled one way or the other, then you must respect anyone who chooses to adopt a different position in their halachic practice.

May you always seek ways to strengthen your bond with our Father in Heaven!

DAF 15

Parenting Styles

Two friends learning in Slabodka had very different temperaments. One learned nonstop in a focused and productive way, while the other wasted a lot of time and spent more time away from the yeshiva than in the study hall. For years, the Alter of Slabodka lavished attention on the latter student. When the Alter paid a *shivah* visit to the studious young man, the fellow complained about his treatment. The Alter responded, "You find your place in learning, so when you come to me with a question, your intention is to satisfy your unspiritual desire to hear praise. Attention from me at such times would be harmful. Your friend's spirit is outside the walls of the yeshiva. When he comes to me, he comes purely to satisfy the needs of his *yetzer tov*. My job, at those moments, is to meet his spiritual needs."[1]

מֵיתִיבִי רַבִּי שִׁמְעוֹן בֶּן אֶלְעָזָר אוֹמֵר לִיקֵט אֶתְרוֹג עֶרֶב חֲמִשָּׁה עָשָׂר בִּשְׁבָט
עַד שֶׁלֹּא תָבוֹא הַשֶּׁמֶשׁ וְחָזַר וְלִיקֵט מִשֶּׁתָּבוֹא הַשֶּׁמֶשׁ אֵין תּוֹרְמִין וּמְעַשְּׂרִין
מִזֶּה עַל זֶה לְפִי שֶׁאֵין תּוֹרְמִין וּמְעַשְּׂרִין לֹא מִן הֶחָדָשׁ עַל הַיָּשָׁן וְלֹא מִן הַיָּשָׁן
עַל הֶחָדָשׁ הָיְתָה שְׁלִישִׁית נִכְנֶסֶת לִרְבִיעִית שְׁלִישִׁית מַעֲשֵׂר רִאשׁוֹן וּמַעֲשֵׂר
עָנִי רְבִיעִית מַעֲשֵׂר רִאשׁוֹן וּמַעֲשֵׂר שֵׁנִי.

---

1   *Sefer HaMeoros HaGedolim*, cited in Pelcovitz and Pelcovitz, *Balanced Parenting*, p. 34.

47

מַאי שָׁנָא הָתָם דְּקָתָנֵי אִם הָיְתָה שְׁנִיָּה נִכְנֶסֶת לִשְׁלִישִׁית וּמַאי שְׁנָא הָכָא
דְּקָתָנֵי אִם הָיְתָה שְׁלִישִׁית נִכְנֶסֶת לִרְבִיעִית מִילְּתָא אַגַּב אוֹרְחֵיהּ קָא מַשְׁמַע
לָן דְּאֶתְרוֹג קַשְׁיָא לֵיהּ יְדָא וְאַיְידֵי דִּמְמַשְׁמְשִׁי בֵּיהּ כּוּלֵּי עָלְמָא בִּשְׁבִיעִית לָא
טָעֵין פֵּרִי עַד תְּלָת שְׁנִין.

*Rabbi Shimon ben Elazar says: If one picked the fruit of an
esrog tree on the eve of the fifteenth of Shevat before the sun
had set, and then he picked more fruit after sunset, he may not
set aside terumah and tithes from the one for the other, as one
may not set aside terumah and tithes from the new crop for
the old or from the old crop for the new. If he did this when it
was the third year of the Sabbatical cycle going into the fourth
year, the halachah is as follows: From what he picked in the
third year he must set aside the first tithe and poor-man's
tithe, and from what he picked in the fourth year he must set
aside the first tithe and second tithe. What is different, that
there, with regard to one who picked vegetables on the eve of
Rosh Hashanah, it teaches the case when it was the second
year of the Sabbatical cycle going into the third year, whereas
here, dealing with one who was picking the fruit of an esrog
tree, it teaches the case when it was the third year going into
the fourth? It serves to teach us a parenthetical matter, that it
is damaging for an esrog when the tree is handled, and since
everyone handles it in the Sabbatical Year, the tree does not
bear fruit that is fit for eating for another three years.*

In each year of the six-year agricultural cycle leading up to the *shem-
ittah*, one must separate tithes for the Kohen and Levi. In addition, on
the first, second, fourth, and fifth years, one must eat a special tithe
(called *maser sheini*) in Jerusalem. On the third and sixth years, this
tithe is given instead to the poor.

Concerning vegetables, the *Beraisa* teaches: "If one picked vegetables
the day before Rosh Hashanah before sundown and then once again
after sundown…if it was the end of the second year and beginning of
the third, the second-year vegetables picked are subject to regular tithes

and *maser sheini* tithes, but the third-year are subject to regular tithes and poor-man's tithes."[2]

By contrast, concerning an esrog, the *Beraisa* teaches: "If one picked an esrog the day before Tu B'Shevat before sundown and then once again after sundown…if it was the end of the third year and beginning of the fourth, the third-year produce is subject to regular tithes and poor-man's tithes, but the fourth-year produce is subject to regular tithes and *maser sheini* tithes."

The discrepancy between the time of year when these two cases take place is due to the fact that vegetables have their New Year on the first of Tishrei, while fruit have theirs on the fifteenth of Shevat. Each of those dates is the cut-off point to determine what crop belongs to the old year and what crop is the part of the new year. But why does the first *Beraisa* use the transition between years 2 and 3, while the second *Beraisa* switches to years 3 and 4? The first time we encounter a difference in tithing duties is between the 2nd and 3rd years, and so the second *Beraisa* should not have waited the extra year!

The Gemara answers that our Sages are teaching us about the tenderness of the esrog tree. During the Sabbatical year, when the field is a free-for-all, everyone comes in and touches the tree. All this touching negatively impacts the tree's ability to bear fruit and, consequently, it doesn't produce any new fruit for the next three years. Interestingly, no matter how much one touches the vegetable plants, there's no damaging effect, but not so with the esrog tree. If nobody would touch the esrog tree, it would bear fruit immediately. Instead, people ruin its ability to grow and bear fruit by their excessive handling.

Parenting books offer all sorts of opinions about how to raise our children, ranging from totally hands-off to nurturing them to a degree that most would call smothering. Should you be active as a parent, staying on top of your children's homework, meeting with their teachers, choosing their friends? Or should you take a step back and let them grow unimpeded?

---

2   *Rosh Hashanah* 12a.

Shlomo HaMelech writes in *Mishlei*, "Educate each child according to his way."[3] In Hashem's parenting book, there is no one perfect way to raise children. Some are little vegetables that need constant nurture—the kind of children that you must ask whether or not they've done their homework, who their friends are, and what time they're coming home.

Other children are like the esrog tree. Too much handling and the child will not succeed. Excessive attention and the tree won't bear fruit. These children need their space to produce the most beautiful fruit of the field. The Vilna Gaon comments on the verse in *Mishlei* that if we fail to understand the unique nature of a child, he will not internalize the values we are seeking to impart. Consequently, he may act according to the ways we've imposed upon him, but as he grows up, he will often reject those values, since the child never connected with those values to begin with.

The art of parenting is taking the time to figure out the nature of each of your children, and not parenting according to your own personal style but according to what's best for each individual child. Rabbi Yisrael Salanter identified with the struggle many parents face when looking for the right school for their children. No school is perfect for your child, he said. Ideally, we should create a distinct school for each child, as every child is unique. Since that's not possible, the role of a parent is magnified. As a parent, you have a responsibility to fill in the personal child-focused gaps to which the school could not possibly cater.[4]

Hashem entrusted you with His children, because He knows that you have the skill to raise them all exceptionally. May you tune in to what each child needs and watch your children grow up to be incredible *menschen* and sources of *nachas*!

---

3   *Mishlei* 22:6.
4   Pelcovitz and Pelcovitz ibid.

Mistakes Are How We Grow

Yosef is languishing in the pit while his brothers are enjoying their lunch. Suddenly, an opportunity presents itself. A caravan of Midianites is passing by, and Yehudah comes up with an idea. "Let's sell him as a slave," he tells his brothers. They nod to one another in agreement, and Yosef is lifted from the pit and sold into slavery. But, it's not long before the brothers begin to feel resentment toward Yehudah for the rash decision. Indeed, when they return to inform their father that Yosef has disappeared, the reaction is stinging. At that point, Yehudah finds himself distanced from the others and moves away from the family.

He marries a Canaanite woman, who bears him three children. Upon the eldest, Er, reaching marriageable age, he finds him a bride named Tamar. Sadly, Er dies prematurely. His brother, Onan, marries Tamar, but, tragically, he too meets an early demise. Yehudah decides that his youngest son, Shelah, is not ready for marriage, but implores Tamar to wait for him. Time marches on, and Tamar isn't getting any younger, so she decides that she must take matters into her own hands. Disguising herself, she is intimate with Yehudah.

Three months later, Yehudah learns that Tamar is pregnant. Filled with indignation at her failure to wait for his youngest son, he demands that she be put to death. On her way, she discloses to Yehudah the paternity of her child. At the eleventh hour, he stands up before all assembled and acknowledges his impropriety.

This courageous act of *teshuvah* established Yehudah as the leader of the brothers. His newfound bravery and self-awareness would later serve him well. When Yosef, who had become the viceroy of Egypt, threatened to imprison Binyamin, it was Yehudah who risked his own life to save their little brother. And, ultimately, these leadership qualities paved the way for the kings of Israel coming from Yehudah's offspring.

וְאָמַר רַבִּי יִצְחָק לָמָּה תּוֹקְעִין בְּראֹשׁ הַשָּׁנָה לָמָּה תּוֹקְעִין רַחֲמָנָא אָמַר תִּקְעוּ
אֶלָּא לָמָּה מְרִיעִין מְרִיעִין רַחֲמָנָא אָמַר זִכְרוֹן תְּרוּעָה אֶלָּא לָמָּה תּוֹקְעִין
וּמְרִיעִין כְּשֶׁהֵן יוֹשְׁבִין וְתוֹקְעִין וּמְרִיעִין כְּשֶׁהֵן עוֹמְדִין כְּדֵי לְעַרְבֵּב הַשָּׂטָן.
רַשִׁ"י: כדי לערבב—לא ישטין כשישמע ישראל מחבבין את המצות
מסתתמין דבריו.

Rabbi Yitzchak said: Why does one sound a tekiah on Rosh Hashanah? Why do we sound a tekiah? The Merciful One states: "Sound a tekiah!" Rather, why does one sound teruah? Sound a teruah? The Merciful One states: "A memorial of teruah." Rather, why does one sound a tekiah and then a teruah while sitting, and then sound again a tekiah and a teruah while they are standing? In order to confuse the Satan.

Rashi: So that he will not accuse. When he hears that Israel loves mitzvos, his words are confounded.

On Rosh Hashanah in shul, we first sound the shofar before the *Musaf* prayer and then again during the prayer. The initial shofar ceremony is referred to as the *tekios d'meyushav*—the seated blasts, since, although we all rise for the mitzvah, strictly speaking one could sit. The second shofar ceremony is called the *tekios d'me'umad*—the standing blasts, since the shofar is blown while we are standing for the *Musaf* service.

Rosh Hashanah is the Day of Judgment, when the Heavenly Court scrutinizes our actions over the past year and determines the outcome for our year ahead. There are advocating angels that defend our record while the Satan leads the prosecution that presents the case against us.

Rashi explains that Rabbi Yitzchak is saying that due to the second set of shofar blasts the Satan will no longer be able to present his case for the prosecution. When he hears how much the Jewish People love mitzvos—so much so that they've blown the shofar not once but twice—his words become confounded.

The *Hafla'ah* teaches that *teshuvah* stemming from fear of Heaven transforms one's sins into *shegagos*—accidental transgressions. *Teshuvah* stemming from love of God, however, transforms one's sins into merits.[1] Given the Jewish People's love of the mitzvos and their resultant *teshuvah* from love, the Satan is fearful of accusing because the more sins he enumerates, the more potential for merit that will ensue as those sins are transformed!

What is the mechanism of sin-merit transformation? Some people think of it as a magical process. But really, it's rather straightforward and logical. We're all human. No one is perfect. We all make mistakes in life, some of which are excusable, others less so. Either way, though, what's done is done, and it's useless to spend the rest of our life crying over mistakes we've made.

Teshuvah entails remorse over past actions and the resolve to learn from our indiscretions, becoming even stronger and wiser from the experience. The question isn't whether we make mistakes in life. The right question is whether we're prepared to learn from those errors and become better people. If we can learn from our past missteps, then we've transformed those painful, embarrassing deeds into merits. What appeared at the time to be so ill-advised has now become the kernel of our next growth and maturity phase of life.

The *Shem MiShmuel* explains the difference between the seated *tekios* and the standing *tekios*. When we're seated, we appear a little too comfortable. That's when the Satan is ready to pounce. But then we stand up and show him that we're prepared to roll up our sleeves and take him on.[2] What does it mean to take him on? It's the willingness to say we're not going to brush our past iniquities and poor choices under the rug.

---

1   Cited in *Yalkut Gershuni*, cited in *Mesivta*; *Kaftor V'Ferach*.
2   *Shem MiShmuel, Ki Seitzei* 5670.

We're going to embrace them and learn from them. When we "stand up" and face the *"tekios"*—the music—of our past, there's nothing left for the Satan to say.

Yehudah's initial reaction to his mistake of selling Yosef was to slink into the background of Jewish history. The Tamar affair could have become a footnote that would not even have made its way into the Biblical narrative, but Yehudah made the conscious decision that he would not repeat his errors. This time, he would stand up and acknowledge his iniquity. And, in that powerful moment, a potentially tragic character of the Torah became transformed into a leading actor of our people.

When we contemplate our life, remember that Hashem knew the choices we would make even before we made them. Just like a wise parent, He held himself back and allowed us to make mistakes so that we would grow from them. We are a product of our nature, nurture, and every life-decision we've ever made—both the wise ones and the impetuous ones. May you embrace every facet of yourself and become a better, transformed individual!

Atoning for Your Original Sin

Elisha ben Avuyah was known as "Acher," the other one. One of the most famous Jewish apostates, he had been a great Rabbinic leader until, one day, he left the holy path of Torah and mitzvos. What made him leave?

According to one source, he entered the Divine realm and saw the angel Matatro-n engaged in the affairs of the world. That sight led him to question the unity of God.

Another source attributes his departure from the Torah way to a time when he witnessed a young man fall from a tree and die. Why was he in the tree? His father had instructed him to remove the mother bird from the nest before taking the eggs in fulfillment of the mitzvah of *shiluach ha'ken*. The Torah's reward for each of these mitzvos—honoring parents and *shiluach ha'ken*—is long life, and yet, Acher saw the opposite play out before his very own eyes.

בֵּית הַלֵּל אוֹמְרִים וְרַב חֶסֶד מַטֶּה כְּלַפֵּי חֶסֶד הֵיכִי עָבֵיד רַבִּי אֱלִיעֶזֶר אוֹמֵר כּוֹבֵשׁ שֶׁנֶּאֱמַר יָשׁוּב יְרַחֲמֵנוּ יִכְבּוֹשׁ עֲוֹנֹתֵינוּ רַבִּי יוֹסֵי בַּר חֲנִינָא אָמַר נוֹשֵׂא שֶׁנֶּאֱמַר נוֹשֵׂא עָוֹן וְעוֹבֵר עַל פֶּשַׁע תָּנָא דְּבֵי רַבִּי יִשְׁמָעֵאל מַעֲבִיר רִאשׁוֹן רִאשׁוֹן וְכֵן הִיא הַמִּדָּה.

Beis Hillel says: When the Torah states that God is "abundant in kindness," it means that He tilts the scales in favor of kindness. How does He do this? Rabbi Eliezer says: He pushes down on the side of the merits, tipping the scale in their favor, as it is stated, "He will again have compassion upon us; He will push down our iniquities." Rabbi Yosi bar Chanina said: He carries the side of the sins, as it is stated, "He bears sin and forgives transgression." The school of Rabbi Yishmael taught: He overlooks each and every first transgression, and that is the attitude toward ensuing sins.

One of the thirteen attributes of God's mercy is that He is "abundant in kindness." The academy of Rabbi Yishmael explains: When an individual is being judged by Heaven, God "removes the first sin, first." Imagine all the merits are on one side of the scale and all the sins on the other. God, in His abundant kindness, extracts the first sin that the person committed and allows the scales to tilt to the side of merit.

How does that work? It makes sense if the merits and sins are more or less equal. Take away one sin, and the scales are now imbalanced in favor of the merit side. But what if the person has many more sins than merits? Simply removing one sin won't achieve anything!

The key to understanding Rabbi Yishmael's statement is in the fact that God is removing the *first* sin. Oftentimes, it's that first sin that leads the person astray. At that critical juncture, the individual was tested. Exercising his free will, he unfortunately chose to sin. What then happens, though, is that he triggers a chain reaction where he ends up committing a slew of further sins in the wake of the first transgression.

The reason that God sees fit to remove the initial sin is that, in reality, that was the only time the person acted of his own volition. All subsequent misbehavior was merely the consequence of his initial sin, and so those sins don't really weigh much on the scales. Remove the big sin, and the scales automatically tip in favor of the side of merit.

That's why our Sages attempt to identify Acher's turning point. If there was one event that they could point to as the cause for his subsequent life-choices, then maybe they could lessen the gravity of Elisha's misdeeds. Removing that first sin would change the entire course of his life. And so, it was really only a single sin or poor judgment of which he was guilty.

Do you ever feel so tied down by your past that you just can't move forward? Many problems that people experience in their lives today are due to deep-seated issues that began way back in their past, and are embedded in their subconscious. If the original point of departure can be mended, the consequences will hopefully fall into place.

The key to improving your relationship with the Almighty is looking back on your life and figuring out the turning point that led you on a path that parted ways with your ideal spiritual direction. If you can pinpoint the decision that you made that triggered your current path, you can work on redirecting yourself toward a different path in life.

Often, it was just one bad decision that led you to where you are today. Don't let one mistake determine the rest of your life! If God can remove that impediment, so can you. Find the fork in the road, backtrack, and take the other path.

And that's not only true of our spiritual lives, but every aspect of our lives. Sometimes, we tell ourselves that it's too late to mend a relationship that's gone sour or a career decision that's taken us down a regrettable path. It might be challenging to backtrack, but going through that temporary pain of taking two steps backwards might change your life for the better in a huge way over the long term.

Maybe it means repeating a year of university to improve your grades. Maybe it means calling up that date from six months ago that didn't go so well because you were in a bad mood that day, apologizing and asking for another chance.

Don't let one mistake or poor judgment call determine your path in life. All you need to do is trace your way back to the initial error and remove it from the scales of life. Sometimes, that's a tough decision to make. But in the long run, it's certainly worth it. May you do your very best to retrace your steps and own the path you take in life!

DAF 18

Banking Your Prayers

Three times a day we daven: morning, afternoon, and evening. These prayers were first recited by our patriarchs, Avraham, Yitzchak, and Yaakov. We daven *Shacharis* because "Avraham arose early in the morning to the place where he had stood." We daven *Minchah* because "Yitzchak went out to communicate (with God) in the field." And, we daven *Maariv* because Yaakov "encountered the place and stayed there overnight for the sun had set."

The Torah does not specify what motivated our forefathers to pray. But Yaakov most certainly had a lot on his mind to pray for at that moment. He had barely escaped the clutches of his brother Eisav, and he was now en route to his uncle, Lavan. As his prayers the following morning demonstrate, Yaakov was worried about what the future held in store.

What was Yitzchak davening for?

תַּנְיָא הָיָה רַבִּי מֵאִיר אוֹמֵר שְׁנַיִם שֶׁעָלוּ לַמִּטָּה וְחוֹלְיָין שָׁוֶה וְכֵן שְׁנַיִם שֶׁעָלוּ לַגַּרְדּוֹם לִידוֹן וְדִינָן שָׁוֶה זֶה יָרַד וְזֶה לֹא יָרַד זֶה נִיצַּל וְזֶה לֹא נִיצַּל מִפְּנֵי מָה זֶה יָרַד וְזֶה לֹא יָרַד זֶה נִיצַּל וְזֶה לֹא נִיצַּל זֶה הִתְפַּלֵּל וְנַעֲנָה וְזֶה הִתְפַּלֵּל וְלֹא נַעֲנָה מִפְּנֵי מָה זֶה נַעֲנָה וְזֶה לֹא נַעֲנָה זֶה הִתְפַּלֵּל תְּפִלָּה שְׁלֵימָה נַעֲנָה וְזֶה לֹא הִתְפַּלֵּל תְּפִלָּה שְׁלֵימָה לֹא נַעֲנָה רַבִּי אֶלְעָזָר אָמַר כָּאן קוֹדֶם גְּזַר דִּין כָּאן לְאַחַר גְּזַר דִּין.

Rabbi Meir would say: Two people take to their beds, and their illness is the same, or two people ascend to the tribunal for

58

judgment, and their potential sentence is the same; but this one descends from his bed, while that one does not descend from his bed, and this one is saved from death, while that one is not saved. For what reason did this one recover and descend from his bed, while that one did not recover and descend from his bed; and why was this one saved, while that one was not saved? The difference is that this one prayed and was answered, while that one prayed, but was not answered. And for what reason was this one answered and that one not answered? This one prayed a complete prayer and was answered, while that one did not pray a complete prayer and, therefore, was not answered. Rabbi Elazar said: Here he prayed before his Heavenly sentence was issued, whereas there the other one prayed after his Heavenly sentence was issued.

Is Rabbi Meir suggesting that if we see someone who does not recover from their illness, it means that he didn't pray hard enough? Had the person prayed a "complete" prayer, would he have survived?

The word "prayer" in English connotes asking God for our needs. *Tefillah*, the Hebrew word for prayer, means so much more. There are various elements of *tefillah*, including praising God, beseeching God, and thanking Him.

The most important function of prayer is connecting with the Almighty. Hashem wants us to have a relationship with Him. The deeper the relationship, the more complete the prayer is and the more complete our relationship with Him is. In fact, the Hebrew word for "complete"—*shalem*—is the same word as "peace"—shalom. To be complete with God is to be at peace with Him.

When you start praying, you expect that God is going to give you the answer that you want to hear. But, the more complete your prayer-experience gets, the more you begin to understand that, ultimately, God knows what's best for us and that if He has decreed a certain fate for us, He knows what He is doing. A complete prayer is one where you develop such an intense relationship with the Almighty that you are completely at peace with His decision.

That's why Rabbi Meir doesn't suggest that the fellow who is "answered" recovers. He may or may not, but he does "leave his bed," i.e., he leaves his predicament with the understanding that Hashem loves him no matter the outcome. Similarly, the one who is "saved" from judgment—whatever the final outcome—he is "saved," knowing that Hashem is in charge of the ultimate plan.

Rabbi Chanoch Gebhard explains the Gemara based on the principle of "preparing the medicine before the illness." Some people only start praying when they face a crisis. When that happens, the prayers are not entirely sincere. Prayer is a conversation with Hashem, incorporating praise, beseeching, and thanks. It's very difficult to praise and thank Hashem when you're in the midst of a crisis, so such a prayer is, inevitably, incomplete.[1]

The individual who was healed was praying to Hashem "before his Heavenly sentence was issued," i.e., before the crisis, meaning to say that he was constantly praying to Hashem long before the crisis hit. Consequently, he was able to pray with the right frame of mind, and the prayer was more complete. Since the prayer wasn't motivated by a crisis, it incorporated all of the necessary elements. Those prayers were then banked, so to speak, and are able to manifest themselves at the time of the crisis.

Prayer is about developing a relationship with the Almighty. Hashem could provide our needs in one lump sum at the beginning of the year. But He wants a daily relationship with each of His children. He wants us to communicate with Him—through the good times and the challenging times. That's the difference between Yitzchak's prayer and Yaakov's. Yitzchak was having a conversation with Hashem, not motivated by any particular crisis. Consequently, our Sages teach that *Minchah*, Yitzchak's prayer, is the most effective.

Prayer is one of the pillars upon which the world stands. It's time to stop thinking about what God can give you or owes you when you talk to Him. Next time you pray, think about everything He already does

---

1   Rabbi Chanoch Gebhard, *Shiurim B'haggados Chazal*, p. 39.

for you. You will be incredibly awestruck and realize how much He loves you.

May you master "complete prayer"—a relationship with the Almighty that transcends the daily ups and downs of your earthly life!

DAF 19

Political Advocacy

Q ueen Esther is about to make the shocking revelation to
Achashverosh that she is a Jewess and that her people have
been targeted for annihilation. To warm him up to the moment,
she invites her husband to a party, and then to a second party.
Strangely, however, she also invites the villain of the story, Haman, to her
parties. Why did Esther find it necessary to invite the wicked Haman?

שֶׁגָּזְרָה מַלְכוּת הָרְשָׁעָה גְּזֵרָה שֶׁלֹּא יַעַסְקוּ בַּתּוֹרָה וְשֶׁלֹּא יָמוּלוּ אֶת בְּנֵיהֶם
וְשֶׁיְּחַלְּלוּ שַׁבָּתוֹת מָה עָשָׂה יְהוּדָה בֶּן שַׁמּוּעַ וַחֲבֵירָיו הָלְכוּ וְנָטְלוּ עֵצָה
מִמַּטְרוֹנִיתָא אַחַת שֶׁכָּל גְּדוֹלֵי רוֹמִי מְצוּיִין אֶצְלָהּ וְאָמְרָה לָהֶם בּוֹאוּ וְהַפְגִּינוּ
בַּלַּיְלָה הָלְכוּ וְהִפְגִּינוּ בַּלַּיְלָה אָמְרוּ אִי שָׁמַיִם לֹא אַחֵיכֶם אֲנַחְנוּ וְלֹא בְּנֵי אָב
אֶחָד אֲנַחְנוּ וְלֹא בְּנֵי אֵם אַחַת אֲנַחְנוּ מָה נִשְׁתַּנֵּינוּ מִכָּל אוּמָּה וְלָשׁוֹן שֶׁאַתֶּם
גּוֹזְרִין עָלֵינוּ גְּזֵירוֹת קָשׁוֹת וּבִיטְלוּם וְאוֹתוֹ הַיּוֹם עֲשָׂאוּהוּ יוֹם טוֹב.

The Roman government once issued a decree against Israel
that they should not occupy themselves with Torah study, and
that they should not circumcise their sons, and that they should
desecrate Shabbos. What did Yehudah ben Shamua and his
colleagues do? They went and took advice from a noblewoman,
whom all the prominent people of Rome would frequent. She
said to them: Come and demonstrate at night. They went and
demonstrated at night, saying, "For Heaven's sake! Are we not
your brothers; are we not children of one father; are we not
children of one mother? How are we different from any other

nation and tongue that you issue such harsh decrees against us?" The decrees were annulled, and they made that day a Yom Tov.

Rabbi Nechemiah teaches that Esther invited Haman so that the Jews would not say, "We have a sister in the palace," and, consequently, not occupy themselves in prayer and *teshuvah*. Her befriending of Haman would cause them to turn their eyes Heavenward in supplication, thinking, "We have no one else to rely upon but our Father in Heaven."[1]

What led to the salvation of the Jewish People from the wicked Haman? Was it Esther's advocacy? Yes. Was it prayer and *teshuvah*? Yes. Both were integral to the redemption. On account of our prayers, God sent salvation through the medium of Esther.

Hashem bids us to seek an earthly blessing to serve as a medium for His *berachah* with every Heavenly blessing that He sends into this world. That's true of work, which creates a vehicle for Hashem's *berachah* of *parnassah*—livelihood. And it's true of our earthly physical and religious rights.

Sadly, it took a couple of generations of persecution before we realized how to work the political system in Rome. Only a few years earlier, Rabbi Shimon bar Yochai was hiding in a cave to learn Torah, and Rabbi Akiva was being martyred for teaching Torah. During that period, we humbly accepted the Divine decree and did what we needed to.

But then, one day, Rabbi Yehudah ben Shamua woke up and wondered, "What if I were to go out and seek advice on how the Roman political system works?" Off he went to a wise lady who explained their system of democracy and that one can transform the system through citizen engagement.

"Go and demonstrate for your rights," she says. "Present your case as a question of religious discrimination and equal rights for all citizens." Sure enough, Rabbi Yehudah and his friends follow her advice, and the laws are changed.

---

1   *Megillah* 15b.

That's why political advocacy for our Jewish communities, as well as for Israel, is so important. Our communities have needs, ranging from Jewish education funding to protection for things like *shechitah* and *bris milah*. To ensure that those freedoms are protected, we must develop and maintain relationships with our elected officials and civil servants. And while Israel is the "land which the eyes of Hashem are constantly upon," He wants us to do our part to create the vessel for His blessing by making our effort to ensure Israel has friends in the global community.

It's important to remember that Hashem doesn't need our help. Rather, in His abundant kindness, He has empowered us with the ability to partner with him in making this world a better place. When Esther responds hesitatingly to Mordechai's appeal to intercede on behalf of the Jewish People, he tells her emphatically, "If you are silent at a time like this, relief and deliverance will arise for the Jews from some other place. Who knows, perhaps it was for a time such as this that you attained royalty?"

Today, we all are royalty. Every one of us has rights and privileges to intercede before the ruling powers, the likes of which our ancestors could only have dreamed of. You have the power of a Moshe Rabbeinu to walk into Pharaoh's palace and make demands for the freedom of your people. You have the power of Esther to walk into Achashverosh's chamber and make demands for the salvation of the Jews. In a certain sense, you are even more powerful than Esther. Unlike Esther, you are not saddled with any fear of retribution as you consider how to make those demands. May you always strive to be a messenger of the Almighty to the ruling powers to guarantee the protection of our religious freedoms and the safety and security of our brothers and sisters in Israel!

DAF 20

Going the Distance on a Three-Day Yom Tov

oward the end of *bentching*, we add in special *Harachamans* on Shabbos and Yom Tov. On Shabbos, we ask Hashem to bequeath us a "Day that is completely Shabbos and restful for all eternity." On Yom Tov, we ask Him to bequeath us a "Day that is completely good." Both are prayers for the speedy ushering in of the Messianic era. What then is the distinction between the two formulas?

כִּי אֲתָא עוּלָּא אָמַר עַבְרוּה לֶאֱלוּל אָמַר עוּלָּא יָדְעִי חַבְרִין בַּבְלָאֵי מַאי טִיבוּתָא עָבְדִינַן בַּהֲדַיְיהוּ טְמָאִי טֵיבוּתָא עוּלָּא אָמַר מְשׁוּם יַרְקָיָא רַבִּי אַחָא בַּר חֲנִינָא אָמַר מְשׁוּם מֵתָיָא מַאי בֵּינַיְיהוּ אִיכָּא בֵּינַיְיהוּ יוֹם הַכִּפּוּרִים שֶׁחָל לִהְיוֹת אַחַר הַשַּׁבָּת מַאן דְּאָמַר מְשׁוּם מֵתָיָא מְעַבְּרִינַן וּמַאן דְּאָמַר מְשׁוּם יַרְקָיָא לְאֵימַת קָא בָּעֵי לְהוּ לְאוֹרְתָּא לְאוֹרְתָּא טָרַח וּמַיְיתֵי וּלְמַאן דְּאָמַר מְשׁוּם יַרְקָיָא לְעַבְרֵיה מְשׁוּם מֵתָיָא אֶלָּא אִיכָּא בֵּינַיְיהוּ יוֹם טוֹב הַסָּמוּךְ לְשַׁבָּת בֵּין מִלְּפָנֶיהָ בֵּין מִלְּאַחֲרֶיהָ מַאן דְּאָמַר מְשׁוּם יַרְקָיָא מְעַבְּרִינַן וּמַאן דְּאָמַר מְשׁוּם מֵתָיָא אֶפְשָׁר בְּעַמְמֵי וּלְמַאן דְּאָמַר מְשׁוּם מֵתָיָא לְעַבְרֵיה מְשׁוּם יַרְקָיָא אֶפְשָׁר בְּחַמִּימֵי.

When Ulla came, he said: This year, they added an extra day to the month of Elul. Ulla continued and said: Do our Babylonian colleagues understand what benefit we did for them? We pushed off Rosh Hashanah for a day so that the Festival would not occur adjacent to Shabbos. The Gemara asks: What is the benefit in having a weekday between Shabbos and a Festival? Ulla said: Due to the vegetables that would not be picked for two days and those picked beforehand that would no longer be fresh. Rabbi Acha bar Chanina said: Due to the dead who would not be buried for two days. What is the difference between these two concerns? If Rosh Hashanah occurs adjacent to Shabbos, either before it or after it. According to the one who said that the reason is due to the vegetables, the court adds an extra day to Elul. But, according to the one who said that the reason is due to the dead, there is no reason to make Elul full, because on a festival it is possible to arrange that the dead be buried by gentiles. But, according to the one who said that the reason is due to the dead, the court should still add an extra day to Elul due to the vegetables! This is not a concern, because it is possible to soak the vegetables in hot water and restore their freshness.

When Ulla arrived from Israel, he told the Babylonians how lucky they were that the High Court in Israel had made a thirty-day month of Elul. "They did you a real favor!" he exclaims.

"What favor?" they ask.

Ulla explains to them that the rabbis made an effort to set the calendar such that they wouldn't have Shabbos and Yom Tov back-to-back. This way, they'd be able to eat fresh vegetables. Otherwise, without refrigeration, they'd go bad after a couple of days.

Rabbi Acha the son of Chanina demurs: "Actually," he announces, "the rabbis are trying to avoid us having Shabbos and Yom Kippur back-to-back so that we don't have any dead bodies lying around awaiting burial for a couple of days!" The Talmud clarifies why Rabbi Acha doesn't go with Ulla's explanation: true, the vegetables might not last if you left them out for a couple of days, but you could always refresh them by soaking them in warm water.

The Shabbos "gift of rest" is an incredible blessing. One day of the week, we get to switch off the chaos of the world around us—no cell-phones, no texting, no email, no Facebook and Twitter updates. One can finally breathe!

For many, it gets to be a little too much when we have a three-day Yom Tov. There's really no such thing as a three-day Yom Tov; the most a Yom Tov can be is two days. But when Yom Tov starts or ends immediately after or before Shabbos, it's possible to have three holy days in a row, which can be pretty demanding on even the most devout.

The challenge of celebrating Shabbos and Yom Tov back-to-back is not a new phenomenon. The rabbis in Jerusalem were aware of the difficulties people experience and did their best to avoid placing us in a situation that some might resent. Shabbos is meant to be pleasurable, and Yom Tov is designed to be joyous. We shouldn't feel that they're a burden.

The fact is that sometimes we do encounter three holy days in succession. Even in Israel, Rosh Hashanah could fall Thursday-Friday and go straight into Shabbos. In order to best approach the proverbial three-day Yom Tov, let's examine the concept of Yom Tov—the "good day."

If you look at the Torah's narrative of the Six Days of Creation, you find that Hashem refers to His creations as "good." What does "good" mean? Anytime we find a word in the Torah, explains the *Ramban*, we must investigate its earliest usage, and that will explain its meaning. The first time we see "good'" is when it refers to the creation of light. This light was not sunlight, as the sun was only created on Day Four. Our Sages teach that the original light was a special light that God kept hidden and reserved for the righteous to utilize.

Light is a tool that is part and parcel of the creative process. When the righteous merit its revelation, they can see "from one end of the world to the other end" and become partners with the Almighty in the building of this world.

How about Shabbos? Is that a "good day?" In contrast with the Days of Creation, God doesn't call the Seventh Day "good." "And God blessed the seventh day, and He sanctified it, because on it, He rested from all His work that God in creating had made." The focus of Shabbos is rest. While the concept of "good" implies engagement in the process of creation, "rest" suggests the removal of oneself from the tumult of the world and carving out a space in time for calmness and tranquility.

That's the difference between the two *Harachaman* prayers we recite in *bentching*. Shabbos is about "rest"—the transformation of oneself into a spiritual being. We leave the craziness of the week behind and allow ourselves time to focus on God, family, and community—all the activities that make us the spiritual beings we are meant to be here on Earth but simply don't have time for throughout the workweek.

Yom Tov is different. It's not about rest and relaxation. "Good" is an aspect of creation. Our Sages teach that Yom Tov is for active engagement. Yom Tov is about eating and drinking (enjoying Hashem's bounty) or going to the *beis midrash*—study hall, to learn Torah. Rabbi Eliezer says that you should pick one of these pastimes to engage in. Rabbi Yehoshua says that you should divide your day between the two and engage in both.[1]

Sadly, when most people get creative, their focus shifts to material pursuits. That's why Hashem had to reserve His special light for the righteous. In the Messianic era, we will all merit to partake of the original light of creation. Nevertheless, Yom Tov is a taste of that light, when even eating and drinking—elevating the pleasures of this world—is a mitzvah.

Shabbos is the time we switch off. Yom Tov is the time we switch on—not our electronic devices or the news ticker, but our spiritual pursuits. On Yom Tov, we learn how to be spiritually creative. You can't simply "be" good. You need to "do" good. And that's the effort we are asked to make each Yom Tov.

Rabbi Acha tells us that we can keep our "little vegetables" fresh by soaking them in warm water. Perhaps, what he means is that you shouldn't assume that your little ones will keep themselves occupied for three days on their own. Especially, in today's electronic age, you need to be creative to keep them excited and engaged. Make time to learn with your children. Go out to the park and have a family picnic on Yom Tov. Prepare a topic for discussion at the table.

---

1   *Pesachim* 68b.

As we approach the Messianic era, it's becoming increasingly challenging to get ourselves and our kids to switch off from the world and become completely focused on spirituality one day each week. It's an even greater challenge to keep the momentum going for two or three days. But with a little planning and creativity, you will wonder where the three days disappeared to; and together with your children, look forward to the next Yom Tov rolling around and begin to yearn for the "Day that is completely good!"

DAF 21

Adapting the Torah for Our Time

fter years eluding capture, Shabbetai the Kid is finally in the court of Shlomo HaMelech. Everyone knows he is guilty. After all, there were multiple sightings of his infamous three-wheeled wagon in the vicinity of a number of sheep thefts. And yet, despite dozens of police interviews, nobody is able to come forward and declare that they'd witnessed Shabbetai in the act of stealing the sheep. Shabbetai is standing in the dock with a disturbing smirk on his face.

What is the king to do? Shlomo, like everyone else in the room, desperately wants a conviction. But there's not enough evidence that any crime has been committed. The king decides that the right thing to do is to take matters into his own hands and issue a unilateral decision.

מָה אֲנִי מְקַיֵּים בְּקֵשׁ קֹהֶלֶת לִמְצוֹא דִּבְרֵי חֵפֶץ בְּקֵשׁ קֹהֶלֶת לָדוּן דִּינִין שֶׁבַּלֵּב שֶׁלֹּא בְעֵדִים וְשֶׁלֹּא בְהַתְרָאָה יָצְתָה בַּת קוֹל וְאָמְרָה לוֹ וְכָתוּב יוֹשֶׁר דִּבְרֵי אֱמֶת עַל פִּי שְׁנַיִם עֵדִים וְגו׳.

What is the meaning of, "Koheles sought to find words of delight?" Koheles sought to issue judgments of the heart (intuitively), without witnesses and without warning. But a Heavenly voice issued forth and said to him, "Yea, the words of truth are inscribed upright." "According to the mouths of two witnesses..."

70

There were many occasions when Shlomo HaMelech desired to avoid due process, including the need for witness testimony and a warning prior to the crime. As the wisest man on Earth, it was only right that he be permitted to adjudicate according to the dictates of his wisdom. But a Heavenly voice issued forth and reminded him that "the words of truth are inscribed upright." The Torah, which is upright and true, makes certain demands of the judicial system.

The Torah has provided us with a system of justice that requires two witnesses, who must undergo detailed cross-examination. If they fail to establish that the defendant is guilty, then the court cannot convict him. It doesn't matter that Shlomo knew the truth. The Torah has spoken. And, ultimately, Shlomo HaMelech had faith that the Almighty is just and that He will take care of the situation.

We are living in spiritually needy times for our people. Before our very eyes, an entire generation of Jews is assimilating away from their Judaism. Forlorn and desperate, we look at our brothers and sisters, and we are driven to do whatever we can to save their souls.

Doing whatever we can, however, must never come at the expense of our holy tradition itself. It's tempting to think that we know better than the Torah. If only we would relax the laws, we tell ourselves, they would come flocking back into the fold of traditional Judaism. If only we would revolutionize and adapt Judaism for the times, our sisters and brothers would be more responsive and interested.

But, then, the mighty Voice issues forth. "Yea, the words of truth are inscribed upright." The Torah is true. It's not for us to overrule or compromise the directives of the Torah and halachah in order to save the Torah. The Almighty has given us the guidebook, and it is our duty to do our very best to draw our brethren near while maintaining an uncompromising commitment to the Torah's tenets.

In *Pirkei Avos*, Hillel teaches, "Be of the students of Aharon. Love peace, pursue peace, love people, and *bring them close to the Torah*." Hillel, the ultimate lover of man and God, reminds us that people must be brought close to the Torah and not the other way around. In our attempt to connect our people to Torah, we mustn't, Heaven forbid, sacrifice the Torah upon the altar of brotherly love.

It might seem obvious to us that certain means will achieve our desired ends. As obvious as the guilt of Shabbetai the Kid appeared to Shlomo HaMelech, he was cautioned that to override the Torah's judicial imperatives is an implicit perversion of justice. Likewise, to bring people closer to Torah by altering the Torah is a self-defeating exercise in futility. It might appear to exhibit temporary benefits, but without the Torah's sanction, it is improper and will not have an enduring positive impact.

Hashem doesn't need His rules to be modified to make it work. Tempting as it is, even if we think we know better, we must maintain the humility that our Heavenly mission is to abide by the Torah within the confines of the Torah. May you forever strive to love people and bring them close to Torah!

Doing Nothing at All Is Sometimes the Hardest Thing to Do

The Baitusim were a Second Temple sect of Jews who didn't believe in the *Torah She'baal Peh*—Oral Law. Not only did they deride the Sages, they would seek ways to undermine traditional Jewish practice, such as the sanctification of the new month. While we have a fixed calendar today, Rosh Chodesh was originally determined by the sighting of the new moon by witnesses, who would travel to the *beis din* in Jerusalem and attest to having seen the moon appear afresh.

On one such occasion, the Baitusim hired two people for four hundred dinars to testify falsely that they had seen the new moon. Unbeknownst to them, however, one of the applicants for the job was a traditional Jew. Off they go to testify, and the first witness, the Baitusi, submits his testimony and leaves.

The traditionalist then enters and the rabbis say to him, "Tell us how you saw the moon."

He replies, "I was ascending Maaleh Adumim, and I saw the new moon crouched between two rocks. Its head was like that of a calf, its ears were like those of a kid, its horns were like those of a deer, and its tail was lying between its thighs. I looked at it and was frightened, and

I fell backward. If you do not believe me, there are two hundred dinars wrapped in my cloak."

They said to him, "Who invited you to testify?"

He said to them, "I heard that the Baitusim were seeking to mislead the Sages, and I said to myself: 'Let me sign up. I will then inform the Sages of this plot. Otherwise, unworthy people will allow their plan to come to its wicked fruition.'"

בָּרִאשׁוֹנָה הָיוּ מְקַבְּלִין עֵדוּת הַחֹדֶשׁ מִכָּל אָדָם וְכוּ' תָּנוּ רַבָּנַן מָה קִלְקוּל קִלְקְלוּ הַבַּייתוֹסִין פַּעַם אַחַת בִּקְּשׁוּ בַּייתוֹסִין לְהַטְעוֹת אֶת חֲכָמִים שָׂכְרוּ שְׁנֵי בְנֵי אָדָם בְּאַרְבַּע מֵאוֹת זוּז אֶחָד מִשֶּׁלָּנוּ וְאֶחָד מִשֶּׁלָּהֶם שֶׁלָּהֶם הֵעִיד עֵדוּתוֹ וְיָצָא שֶׁלָּנוּ אָמְרוּ לוֹ אֱמֹר כֵּיצַד רָאִיתָ אֶת הַלְּבָנָה אָמַר לָהֶם עוֹלֶה הָיִיתִי בְּמַעֲלֶה אֲדוּמִים וּרְאִיתִיו שֶׁהוּא רָבוּץ בֵּין שְׁנֵי סְלָעִים רֹאשׁוֹ דּוֹמֶה לְעֵגֶל אָזְנָיו דּוֹמִין לִגְדִי קַרְנָיו דּוֹמוֹת לִצְבִי וּזְנָבוֹ מוּנַּחַת לוֹ בֵּין יַרְכוֹתָיו וְהֵצַצְתִּי בּוֹ וְנִרְתַּעְתִּי וְנָפַלְתִּי לַאֲחוֹרַי וְאִם אֵין אַתֶּם מַאֲמִינִים לִי הֲרֵי מָאתַיִם זוּז צְרוּרִין לִי בִּסְדִינִי אָמְרוּ לוֹ מִי הִזְקִיקְךָ לְכָךְ אָמַר לָהֶם שָׁמַעְתִּי שֶׁבִּקְּשׁוּ בַּייתוֹסִים לְהַטְעוֹת אֶת חֲכָמִים אָמַרְתִּי אֵלֵךְ אֲנִי וְאוֹדִיעַ לָהֶם שֶׁמָּא יָבוֹאוּ בְּנֵי אָדָם שֶׁאֵינָם מְהוּגָּנִין וְיַטְעוּ אֶת חֲכָמִים אָמְרוּ לוֹ מָאתַיִם זוּז נְתוּנִין לְךָ בְּמַתָּנָה וְהַשּׂוֹכֵר יִמָּתַח עַל הָעַמּוּד בְּאוֹתָהּ שָׁעָה הִתְקִינוּ שֶׁלֹּא יְהוּ מְקַבְּלִין אֶלָּא מִן הַמַּכִּירִין.

Initially, they would accept testimony to determine the start of the month from any person. But then, the Sages saw that the Baitusim were engaging in destructive practices. What were they? On one occasion, the Baitusim hired two people for four hundred dinars to testify falsely...The Sages said to him: The two hundred dinars are given to you as a gift. And the one who hired you shall be punished. Then and there, the Sages instituted that they would accept only from those with whom they were acquainted.

What was bothering the Baitusim? What was motivating their desire to undermine the *beis din*? Granted, they didn't hold traditional Jewish beliefs, but why couldn't they simply practice their Judaism as they saw fit? Why did they feel the need to disrupt mainstream Jewish observance?

The issue we see here is one that arises time and again. Many individuals and groups that break away from tradition are terribly uncomfortable with the persistence of traditional Jewish practice and devotees. The most tragic example of this phenomenon is the attitude of Christianity toward Judaism for the better part of two millennia. Despite the fact that Christian adherents far outnumbered the Jewish People, our continued presence and dedication to Torah and mitzvos was a thorn in their eye. "If we're the new Hebrews," they thought, "why are the old Hebrews still here? If God has abrogated our obligation to observe the commandments, why are the Jews still practicing?" For the most part, Christians don't openly persecute and destroy our people and tradition as they once did.

While intolerant people are no longer burning others at the stake, the newest incarnation of this phenomenon is "Cancel Culture." Rather than simply agreeing to disagree, some people are so bothered by those who hold opinions contrary to theirs that they feel the need to attack them personally and undermine their very existence.

If one is comfortable with one's own beliefs, there's no need to attack others. The Rabbis never attempted to act with stealth and mischief to undermine Baitusi practice; they respected their Divine right to free choice. As long as the traditionalists continued engaging in their "antiquated" ways, however, the Baitusim could not rest. They thought of themselves as progressive and open-minded, but their open-mindedness led to intolerance of, and antagonism toward, those whom they considered close-minded.

If you are being attacked and undermined personally for your convictions and way of life, it's a tell-tale sign that you are doing the right thing. If you haven't provoked the attacks, then it's just a case of Baitusi jealousy. It's tempting to want to fight back and attack your critics personally, but you don't need to do that. You can argue and debate ideas, if you feel that such engagement might bear fruit. But the second that it becomes personal, run in the opposite direction. Ad hominem attacks are only for the weak and jealous.

Don't let the naysayers get you down. You know you're doing the right thing. You know you're keeping company with the right crowd. Doing the right thing is a big mitzvah, but not doing anything when you're being mistreated is an even bigger mitzvah. May you forever hold your head high and maintain the courage to stick to your convictions, and may Hashem reward you for all your efforts, especially all the times you did nothing!

DAF 23

The Duty to Share Torah

Rabbi Yosi ben Kisma, the great Mishnaic sage, was once traveling through the countryside, when he encountered a fellow with an offer he almost couldn't refuse.

"Shalom!" the fellow said.

"Shalom!" responded Rabbi Yosi.

"Rabbi, where are you from?" the man asked.

Rabbi Yosi replied, "I'm from a great city of scholars and sages."

"Would you like to come and live with us in our place?" inquired the fellow. "I'd be willing to give you thousands upon thousands of gold coins, precious stones, and pearls."

"Even if you were to give me all the silver, gold, precious stones, and pearls in the world," the rabbi responded, "I would only live in a place of Torah!"[1]

וְאָמַר רַבִּי יוֹחָנָן כָּל הַלּוֹמֵד תּוֹרָה וְאֵינוֹ מְלַמְּדָהּ דּוֹמֶה לַהֲדַס בַּמִּדְבָּר אִיכָּא דְּאָמְרִי כָּל הַלּוֹמֵד תּוֹרָה וּמְלַמְּדָהּ בִּמְקוֹם שֶׁאֵין תַּלְמִידֵי חֲכָמִים דּוֹמֶה לַהֲדַס בַּמִּדְבָּר דְּחָבִיב.

Rabbi Yochanan said: Anyone who studies Torah but does not teach it to others is likened to a myrtle in the wilderness. There are those who say: Anyone who studies Torah and teaches it

---

1   *Avos* 6:9.

77

> *to others in a place where there are no other Torah scholars is*
> *likened to a myrtle in the wilderness, which is precious.*

To paraphrase Rabbi Yochanan's teaching: If a myrtle grows in the desert and no one is there to smell it, does it have a fragrance? The alternate teaching suggests that a myrtle is only a myrtle when there are people around who are able to enjoy its fragrance. In fact, the *Maharsha* explains that a myrtle growing in the wilderness imparts a more distinct fragrance than a myrtle found in a field of myrtle branches.

So, if indeed it is praiseworthy to teach Torah in the wilderness, why was Rabbi Yosi ben Kisma hesitant upon being invited to move to the "country?"

The problem with that particular fellow was that he was asking the rabbi to simply "live with us in our place." He wasn't asking to learn Torah or that the rabbi should establish a yeshiva in their city. He just wanted the *kavod* of having Rabbi Yosi as their figurehead.

The Gemara teaches that there are two ways to be a myrtle. Either you live amongst Torah scholars, or you go out into the spiritual desert and teach Torah. Living out in the desert and not teaching Torah is not an option, even for all the money in the world.

So, if you find yourself living outside the Torah centers of the world, you have two choices. Either you move to a "great city of scholars and sages," or you start teaching Torah to those around you. As little as you might think you know, there are others out there in your community who know even less. If you know an *alef* and a *beis*, and someone out there only knows an *alef*, you have a duty to teach him the *beis*!

Even if you are living in a scholarly city, that doesn't mean you're not duty-bound. By teaching Torah even when there are others already engaged in Torah education, you become a super-myrtle. Your fragrance becomes unforgettable. There's not a place in the world that's oversaturated with Torah teachers. There's always someone you can find to whom you can teach Torah. Maybe it's a struggling neighbor's child. Maybe it's your local corner-store owner. Maybe it's your own child who could do with a little extra attention and focus.

The Gemara's message is that it doesn't matter where you are. What matters is whether or not you choose to spread the sweet fragrance of Torah. If you are in the desert, the Almighty has planted you there to become a myrtle. And if you're in the city, in a certain sense, the challenge of being a myrtle is even greater. May your fragrance spread far and wide!

DAF 24

Keeping Our Eyes Safe

A side from being the wisest man in Egypt, a pious, God-fearing individual, and a dream interpreter beyond compare, Yosef also happened to be incredibly handsome. It wasn't only Potiphar's wife who admired his beauty, all the maidens of the land sought to catch a glimpse of the viceroy. When Yaakov later blessed his son, he commented that the Egyptian ladies were known to stand upon the city wall so that they could climb up and peer over at Yosef.

תָּנוּ רַבָּנָן רְאִינוּהוּ וְשׁוּב לֹא רְאִינוּהוּ אֵין מְעִידִין עָלָיו כָּל הָכִי חָזוּ לֵהּ וְאָזְלִי אָמַר אַבַּיֵי הָכִי קָאָמַר רְאִינוּהוּ מֵאֵלֵינוּ וְשַׁבְנוּ לִרְאוֹתוֹ מִדַּעְתֵּנוּ וְלֹא רְאִינוּהוּ אֵין מְעִידִין עָלָיו מַאי טַעְמָא אֵימוֹר כּוֹבִיתָא דְעֵיבָא בְּעָלְמָא הוּא דְחָזֵי.

If the witnesses say: "One moment we saw the new moon, but then we did not see it again," they may not testify about it. But must they then continue to watch it? Abaye said that this is the meaning. If the witnesses say: "We saw the moon randomly, and then we returned to look for it on purpose, but we did not see it again," they may not testify about it. What is the reason? Because one can say that it was merely a small round white cloud that they saw.

In Temple times, the new month was determined by the sighting of the new moon. Each month, the High Court waited for witnesses to arrive to pronounce the new month. One time, they came to the court and testified that they had seen the moon and subsequently didn't see it. In such a situation, the *Beraisa* teaches that we don't accept their testimony. Why not? Isn't it enough just to see it one time?

Abaye explains that their meaning is that they happened to notice the moon unconsciously, and then they took another conscious look and failed to see it. In this case, we assume that what they'd seen out of the corner of their eyes the first time was just the arc of a cloud. Sometimes we see something, and then we need to take a second look just to confirm what we saw the first time.

In the third paragraph of the *Shema* prayer, we say "You shall not stray after your hearts and after your eyes." Isn't that the wrong way around? First you see something improper and then your heart chooses whether to stray after it. It should say, "You shall not stray after your eyes and after your hearts!"

There's a difference between unconscious and conscious sight. Your eyes are constantly seeing things around you. Once the eyes have spotted something, they send a message to the brain, which registers what they've seen. That's what's happening with our witnesses who saw the moon. They saw something out of the corner of their eyes that looked like the moon. Upon registering that they'd caught a glimpse of the moon, they refocused and took another look.

Your eyes encounter all sorts of stimuli just by walking down the street or turning on the internet. Most of that stimuli you can't really control. But when you see something inappropriate out of the corner of your eye, which then registers in your mind, at that point, you get to control what happens next.

Your heart will try to convince you to take a better look. That second look is the conscious look. You're not culpable for the first glance; that was beyond your control. It's the second look that gets you in trouble. That's why the verse reads, "You shall not stray after your hearts and after your eyes." The heart desires and then the eyes take another look.

Nobody is immune from the stimuli that surround us on a continual basis. Our Sages were even concerned about the young Kohanim serving in the Temple that they wouldn't be able to remove the thoughts that entered their minds upon witnessing the *Sotah* ritual. The Gemara says that once you've gazed at something, the *yetzer hara* seizes the moment to maintain that image.[1]

Of course, the Kohanim were in the course of their Temple service, and so there was only so much that could be done to avoid any negative impacts of what they saw. The issue is when we consciously "climb the wall" to gaze at things toward which we shouldn't be turning our attention.

It's not easy today to control what your eyes see. Inappropriate images abound and, today, immodest attire is the norm. You have the choice whether or not to take that second look. May your mind always control your heart's desire to control your eyes!

---

1   *Sotah* 8a.

Shalom Bayis Is More Important than Being Right

n Temple times, the new month was determined by the sighting of the new moon. Each month, the High Court waited for witnesses to arrive to pronounce the new month. One time, they came to the court and testified before Rabban Gamliel that they had seen the moon on the correct day, but not in the subsequent evening, and Rabban Gamliel nonetheless accepted their testimony.

Rabbi Dosa ben Horkinus dissented, "They are false witnesses!" he cried, "How can one testify that a woman gave birth, and the next day we see her still pregnant?" Rabbi Yehoshua agreed.

Rabban Gamliel sent a message to Rabbi Yehoshua: "I hereby decree that you shall appear before me with your staff and wallet on the day Yom Kippur occurs according to your calculation!"

הָלַךְ וּמְצָאוֹ רַבִּי עֲקִיבָא מֵיצֵר אָמַר לוֹ יֵשׁ לִי לִלְמוֹד שֶׁכָּל מַה שֶּׁעָשָׂה רַבָּן
גַּמְלִיאֵל עָשׂוּי שֶׁנֶּאֱמַר אֵלֶּה מוֹעֲדֵי ה׳ מִקְרָאֵי קֹדֶשׁ אֲשֶׁר תִּקְרְאוּ אֹתָם בֵּין
בִּזְמַנָּן בֵּין שֶׁלֹּא בִּזְמַנָּן אֵין לִי מוֹעֲדוֹת אֶלָּא אֵלּוּ בָּא לוֹ אֵצֶל רַבִּי דוֹסָא בֶּן
הוֹרְכִּינַס אָמַר לוֹ אִם בָּאִין אָנוּ לָדוּן אַחַר בֵּית דִּינוֹ שֶׁל רַבָּן גַּמְלִיאֵל צְרִיכִין
אָנוּ לָדוּן אַחַר כָּל בֵּית דִּין וּבֵית דִּין שֶׁעָמַד מִימוֹת מֹשֶׁה וְעַד עַכְשָׁיו שֶׁנֶּאֱמַר
וַיַּעַל מֹשֶׁה וְאַהֲרֹן נָדָב וַאֲבִיהוּא וְשִׁבְעִים מִזִּקְנֵי יִשְׂרָאֵל וְלָמָּה לֹא נִתְפָּרְשׁוּ
שְׁמוֹתָן שֶׁל זְקֵנִים אֶלָּא לְלַמֵּד שֶׁכָּל שְׁלֹשָׁה וּשְׁלֹשָׁה שֶׁעָמְדוּ בֵּית דִּין עַל

יִשְׂרָאֵל הֲרֵי הוּא כְּבֵית דִּינוֹ שֶׁל מֹשֶׁה נָטַל מַקְלוֹ וּמְעוֹתָיו בְּיָדוֹ וְהָלַךְ לְיַבְנֶה
אֵצֶל רַבָּן גַּמְלִיאֵל בַּיּוֹם שֶׁחָל יוֹם הַכִּפּוּרִים לִהְיוֹת בְּחֶשְׁבּוֹנוֹ עָמַד רַבָּן גַּמְלִיאֵל
וּנְשָׁקוֹ עַל רֹאשׁוֹ אָמַר לוֹ בּוֹא בְּשָׁלוֹם רַבִּי וְתַלְמִידִי רַבִּי בְּחָכְמָה וְתַלְמִידִי
שֶׁקִּבַּלְתָּ אֶת דְּבָרִי.

Rabbi Akiva went and found Rabbi Yehoshua distressed. He said to him: I can learn from a verse that everything that Rabban Gamliel did is valid. As it is stated: "These are the appointed seasons of the Lord, sacred convocations, which you shall proclaim." Whether you have proclaimed them at their proper time or whether you have declared them not at their proper time, I have only these Festivals as established by the representatives of the Jewish People. Rabbi Yehoshua then came to Rabbi Dosa ben Horkinas, who said to him: If we were to debate the rulings of the court of Rabban Gamliel, then we would have to question the rulings of every court that has stood from the days of Moshe until now. As it is stated: "Then Moshe went up, and Aharon, Nadav, and Avihu, and seventy of the Elders of Israel." But why were the names of these seventy Elders not specified? Rather, this comes to teach that every set of three judges that stands as a court over the Jewish People has the same status as the court of Moshe. Upon hearing this, he took his staff and his money in his hand, and went to Yavneh to Rabban Gamliel on the day on which Yom Kippur occurred according to his own calculation. Upon seeing him, Rabban Gamliel stood up and kissed him on his head. He said to him: Come in peace, my teacher and my student. You are my teacher in wisdom, and you are my student, as you accepted my statement.

While Rabbi Dosa didn't agree with Rabban Gamliel's ruling, he recognized the danger of public dissent. Rabban Gamliel presided over the Sanhedrin, and if we wouldn't accept their ruling, why should we accept any prior *beis din*'s rulings? One might not agree with everything in halachah. One might even think that the Rabbis have confused which day is Yom Kippur. Nevertheless, the way the system works is that

Hashem entrusted our Sages with the important task of maintaining our heritage and the halachic process.

That requires considerable humility. Rabbi Yehoshua knew that he was right, but although he may have been factually correct, he was practically wrong. When it comes to practice, our tradition values uniformity over accuracy and, one might say, even truth. In Hebrew, we would define this prioritization as *shalom* over *emes*. The uniformity of halachic practice is a form of peace-keeping. The *emes*—at least as far as Rabbi Yehoshua saw things—was that he should not wander about on his Yom Kippur with his staff in his hand. But his colleagues persuaded him that the *middah* of *shalom* was more important.

That's the case not just in matters of halachah but in many aspects of our lives. Let's say you've had a disagreement with someone with whom you're close. Maybe it's your spouse. You know that you're right. Again. It's really only a matter of time before she realizes how right you are. At the moment, you're convinced that she's just being stubborn.

You could continue to stand on ceremony until she comes around to your way of seeing things. But most of the time, it really is not worth it. The humble decision to pick up your staff and demonstrate your surrender to the other spouse's position might just be the right decision for the success of the relationship. Which would you prefer: being right or being married?

So many of the arguments that we have with our loved ones, colleagues, neighbors, and community members are fairly inconsequential. Most of them certainly are not on the level of carrying on Yom Kippur, which is what Rabbi Yehoshua had to do to demonstrate his commitment to Rabban Gamliel. And yet he did it, because there was significantly more at stake than proving that he was right.

Obviously, even this principle has limits. If your spouse said, "Let's stop keeping Shabbos," or "A Jewish education is not important for our children," those would be red lines. But, sadly, far too many disagreements in which we engage with our loved ones are petty and inconsequential. It doesn't necessarily make it any easier to humbly give in, but the question you must always ask yourself is: What's more important to me right now—winning the argument or strengthening my relationship?

No two individuals are of the same mind in every situation. Therefore, all relationships require humility. May you forever strive to maintain *shalom* as the ultimate value in your life!

Speech Mastery Is a Prerequisite for Prayer

One year, prior to Pesach, the Chafetz Chaim visited a certain town. Upon meeting with the community leaders, they began bemoaning the fact that the *maos chittim*—donations for poor families—were significantly down that year and that they had insufficient funds to distribute. The Chafetz Chaim listened to their concerns and offered to do whatever he could to help.

"Would their illustrious visitor address the community on their behalf?" they wondered aloud.

"Of course," replied the Chafetz Chaim.

That evening, the community members filled the shul, and the Chafetz Chaim declared:

"I am already an old man. We all know I won't live forever. When I arrive and stand before the Heavenly court, they will ask me whether sufficient *maos chittim* were provided in your community. When we get to that question, I will find myself in a quandary.

"On the one hand, if I respond affirmatively, saying that you gave all you were able to give, that will be a lie. Would anyone here think for a moment that I could ever utter a falsehood? And before the Heavenly court, on top of it! On the other hand, if I respond to their question negatively and say that you didn't give enough, that will be *lashon hara*!

I've spent my whole life distancing myself from *lashon hara*; would I start now by speaking ill of an entire community?"

The Chafetz Chaim began to cry, but then he continued. "Therefore, I beg of this holy congregation: Save me from this terrible predicament. I need you to please give *maos chittim* generously!"

And sure enough, that year, the needy members of the community ate to their heart's content—Pesach feasts fit for kings and queens![1]

מַתְנִי׳ כָּל הַשּׁוֹפָרוֹת כְּשֵׁרִים חוּץ מִשֶּׁל פָּרָה: גְּמִ׳ עוּלָּא אָמַר הַיְינוּ טַעְמָא
דְּרַבָּנָן כִּדְרַב חִסְדָּא דְּאָמַר רַב חִסְדָּא מִפְּנֵי מָה אֵין כֹּהֵן גָּדוֹל נִכְנָס בְּבִגְדֵי
זָהָב לִפְנַי וְלִפְנִים לַעֲבוֹד עֲבוֹדָה לְפִי שֶׁאֵין קָטֵיגוֹר נַעֲשָׂה סָנֵיגוֹר.

רש״י: אין קטיגור—זהב העגל ושופר של פרה נמי קטיגור דעגל הוא.

Mishnah: All shofars are fit for blowing except for the horn of a cow. Gemara: Ulla said: This accords with Rav Chisda's teaching, for Rav Chisda taught: For what reason does the High Priest not enter the innermost sanctum, the Holy of Holies, with his golden garments to perform the service there on Yom Kippur? It is because a prosecutor cannot become a defender.

Rashi: The gold of the calf, and likewise a cow's horn, is a prosecutor for its calf.

Ulla explains that the problem with using a cow's horn is that it is reminiscent of the golden calf. On the High Holy days, we seek atonement. It would be inappropriate to appear before Hashem with symbols of our past iniquities and expect to be forgiven. Ulla derives his understanding from Rav Chisda's similar teaching about the Kohen Gadol who, throughout the year, wears gold vestments. On Yom Kippur, however, he wears white, so as to avoid any reference to the golden calf incident, since gold, which is "the prosecutor, cannot become the defender."

The *Chayei Adam* writes that the mouth, tongue, lips, and teeth correspond to the four priestly garments.[2] If the Kohen's clothes were sullied, he could not perform his holy service. Likewise, if the mouth is

---

1   *Chashukei Chemed, Haggadah shel Pesach*, p. 4.
2   *Chayei Adam* 143. See also *Shu"t Beis Halevi*, vol. 2, *derush* 15.

sullied with improper speech, our ability to converse with Hashem in prayer—our *avodah*—is impeded because a prosecutor cannot become a defender.

Sometimes, when we think about improper speech, the primary matter that comes to mind is the sin of *lashon hara*. However, the Chafetz Chaim lists ten ways that we can sully our mouths:

1. *Lashon hara* (gossip)
2. *Rechilus* (reporting gossip back)
3. *Onaah* (insults)
4. Embarrassing another person
5. Lying
6. Cursing another person
7. Arrogant talk
8. Quarrelsome speech
9. *Chanufah* (sycophancy)
10. Angry outbursts[3]

Each of these areas requires conscious efforts to improve our negative habits and perfect our behavior. Some people struggle with some of these character flaws. Others find different ones more challenging. We all have abundant room for growth and improvement in the area of speech.

But in the meantime, how is anyone able to pray, so long as we have not yet perfected our mouths and readied them for prayer?

The Vilna Gaon teaches that sharing words of Torah has the power to purify one's mouth of the defilement of *lashon hara*.[4] It is certainly no substitute for the long, hard battle with the *yetzer hara* for mastery over the ten areas of speech imperfection. In the short-term, however, it serves as a quick rinse to allow for the beginning of a conversation with the Almighty.

Speech is one of the most challenging areas of personal character refinement to master, but you can do it. If the Almighty has challenged

---

3   Cited in Pliskin, *Consulting the Wise*, 15:1.
4   Ibid. 1:46.

you in a particular area of speech, He has also given you the power to overcome your challenge. May you utilize your mouth to declare the praises of God in this world!

DAF 27

Listen before You Speak

hanah has been longing for a child ever since she married Elkanah many years ago.

"But you are more precious to me than all the sons and daughters in the world!" her husband tells her, trying to cheer her up.

She is unwilling to be consoled. So, off she goes to the Tabernacle to pour out her heart before God.

She enters the Tabernacle, turns her eyes Heavenward, and offers a fervent and passionate prayer, the likes of which has not ever been witnessed by the Kohanim on duty.

Eli the Kohen Gadol assumes she is not entirely sober. He begins to berate her for entering the Holy Tabernacle in a state of drunkenness.

Chanah does not raise her voice in response. She stands there quietly listening to his condemnation. At the conclusion of his stern lecture, she gently explains to him that she is not drunk but is praying from the depths of her soul for a child.

Eli blesses her and, sure enough, she conceives and bears a child, who would grow to become one of the greatest prophets that our people has ever seen—Shmuel HaNavi.

מתני׳ שׁוֹפָר שֶׁל רֹאשׁ הַשָּׁנָה שֶׁל יָעֵל פָּשׁוּט וּפִיו מְצוּפֶּה זָהָב וּשְׁתֵּי חֲצוֹצְרוֹת
מִן הַצְּדָדִין שׁוֹפָר מַאֲרִיךְ וַחֲצוֹצְרוֹת מְקַצְרוֹת שֶׁמִּצְוַת הַיּוֹם בְּשׁוֹפָר.

וּתְרֵי קָלֵי מִי מִשְׁתַּמְעִי וְהָתַנְיָא זָכוֹר וְשָׁמוֹר בְּדִיבּוּר אֶחָד נֶאֶמְרוּ מַה שֶׁאֵין
הַפֶּה יְכוֹלָה לְדַבֵּר וְאֵין הָאוֹזֶן יְכוֹלָה לִשְׁמוֹעַ לְכָךְ מַאֲרִיךְ בְּשׁוֹפָר.

91

Mishnah: The shofar used on Rosh Hashanah in the Temple was made from the straight horn of an ibex, and its mouthpiece was golden. And there were two trumpets, one on each of the two sides. The shofar would sound a long blast, whereas the trumpets would sound a short blast, because the mitzvah of the day is with the shofar.

Gemara: But is it really possible to discern two different sounds at the same time? Isn't it taught that "Remember Shabbos" and "Keep Shabbos" were spoken in a single utterance, something that the human mouth cannot speak and the human ear cannot hear? That is why they would sound a long blast with the shofar.

David HaMelech writes in *Tehillim*, "With trumpets and the sound of a shofar, you shall blow before Hashem, the King." From here we learn that in the Temple, trumpets accompanied the sound of the shofar. The Gemara asks, "Can two sounds be heard at the same time?" If we are required to hear the sound of the shofar to fulfill our Rosh Hashanah obligation, then the extra sound of the trumpets would impede our ability to hear the shofar clearly. Therefore, the shofar sound must continue beyond the shofar blasts.

Our Sages teach that just like no two people have the same face, similarly no two people have the same opinions. All relationships are about bringing in the ideas of other people into your own mind-space. The ultimate relationship and thought-sharing takes place, of course, in marriage. But, as the Talmud points out, generally you can't comprehend two sounds at the same time. If you desire a meaningful relationship with your spouse or any other person, you must be prepared to listen. Once he has spoken his mind, then you can have your turn.

When a wife accuses her spouse, saying that her words are going "in one ear and out the other," what does she mean? I think about the couple who came to me for marriage counseling.

"He never listens to me," she said.

"She never listens to me," he seemed to say at exactly the same moment.

I tried to say something, but each one was getting louder and louder as they tried to speak over the other one.

People will often hear the words that their spouse is saying, but won't stop to process them. They've "listened" while their own voice inside their head was still screaming. You can't do that. Two voices can't be heard at once. You need to let go of your own voice and listen to the other person.

A debating tip that I teach many young couples is to listen to their spouse and then say, "So what you're saying is…" Invariably, the spouse will say, "No, that's not what I said. I meant…" And I'll encourage them to try again to repeat what their spouse said. Once you can repeat the message and confirm that you've understood, then your spouse knows that you're actually listening. That's step one in resolving a disagreement—acknowledgment and understanding of the other person's position.

And that's true of all relationships and dialogue. We need to stop and listen. Pay attention to what the other person is saying. Take it in. Try and repeat in your own words what the other person is saying. Then you can respond with your perspective.

Chanah could have tried to stop Eli's criticism, but it would have turned into a shouting match, as each tried to talk over the other one, claiming to be correct and that the other person suffered from poor judgment. The only thing that it would have achieved would have been her eviction from the Tabernacle. Instead, she listened calmly to him, taking in everything he was saying. When he had finished speaking his mind, she was then ready to respond. The exchange ended with blessings.

Two sounds can't be processed at the same time. Unless you can clear your mind and listen, you'll never be able to appreciate what anyone else has to offer. First things first, you need to let the other party have his say and be able to repeat and validate his concerns. Only then can you express your measured and thoughtful response. May you master the art of the single voice of resolution!

DAF 28

Mitzvos beyond Your Comfort Zone

Avraham was ninety-nine years old, and Hashem appeared to him to make a covenant—not of mere words but of the flesh. He and his descendants would circumcise themselves for all generations. Avraham, the servant of Heaven, complies with this enormous demand unhesitatingly. He is in the midst of recovering from this incredible physical ordeal when Hashem appears to him. He begins to reveal the next phase of the Divine plan when Avraham stops Him, mid-sentence.

"Excuse me, Father in Heaven, I see some men approaching in the distance." Sure enough, three men were making their way toward Avraham and Sarah's wilderness tent. Our patriarch and matriarch were the epitome of hospitality. Not even a conversation with the Almighty Himself could prevent them from fulfilling the mitzvah of *hachnasas orchim*, bringing in guests. And indeed, from this incident, our Sages derive, "Bringing in guests is greater than receiving the Divine presence."

אָמַר רַב יְהוּדָה בְּשׁוֹפָר שֶׁל עוֹלָה לֹא יִתְקַע וְאִם תָּקַע יָצָא בְּשׁוֹפָר שֶׁל שְׁלָמִים לֹא יִתְקַע וְאִם תָּקַע לֹא יָצָא מַאי טַעְמָא עוֹלָה בַּת מְעִילָה הִיא כֵּיוָן דִּמְעַל בַּהּ נָפְקָא לַהּ לְחוּלִּין שְׁלָמִים דְּלָאו בְּנֵי מְעִילָה נִינְהוּ אִיסּוּרָא הוּא דִּרְכִיב בְּהוּ וְלָא נָפְקִי לְחוּלִּין מַתְקֵיף לַהּ רָבָא אֵימַת מָעַל לְבָתַר דְּתָקַע כִּי קָא תָקַע בְּאִיסּוּרָא תָּקַע אֶלָּא אָמַר רָבָא אֶחָד זֶה וְאֶחָד זֶה לֹא יָצָא הַדַּר אָמַר רָבָא אֶחָד זֶה וְאֶחָד זֶה יָצָא מִצְוֹת לָאו לֵיהָנוֹת נִיתְּנוּ.

רש״י: לא ליהנות ניתנו—לישראל להיות קיומם להם הנאה אלא לעול
על צואריהם ניתנו.

*Rav Yehudah said: One should not blow with the shofar of an
animal consecrated as an Olah offering, but if he nevertheless
transgressed and blew, he has fulfilled his obligation. One
should also not blow with the shofar of an animal consecrated
as a peace-offering, and if he nevertheless transgressed and
blew, he has not fulfilled his obligation. What is the reason
for this distinction? An Olah offering is subject to the law of
misappropriation, and once one uses it for mundane purposes,
it becomes non-sacred, so that the one who blows with its
shofar fulfills his obligation. In contrast, peace-offerings are
not subject to the law of misappropriation. Therefore, the
prohibition remains intact and they do not become non-sacred.
Rava objected: When does he commit misappropriation? After
he has sounded it, for only then has he misused the consecrated
animal. If so, when he sounds it, he is sounding with something
that is still prohibited. Consequently, Rava said: In both cases,
he has not fulfilled his obligation. Later, Rava said: In both
cases, he has fulfilled his obligation, for mitzvos were not given
for enjoyment.*

*Rashi: They were not given to Israel to derive enjoyment from
their fulfillment. Rather, they were placed as a yoke upon their
necks.*

One is not allowed to use property that was consecrated for use in
the Beis Hamikdash. How about blowing the shofar with the horn of
an animal that was designated to be offered as a sacrifice? Rav Yehudah
contrasts two Temple offerings: One should not blow with a shofar
taken from the horn of an *Olah* offering, but, if he did blow, he has
fulfilled his obligation. One should not blow with a shofar taken from
the horn of a *Shelamim* (peace) offering, but if he did blow, he has not
fulfilled his obligation.

What is the difference between these two offerings? An *Olah* offering
is subject to the law of *me'ilah*, which says that if one derived benefit

from something that was consecrated for the Temple, he deconsecrates the item and must compensate the Temple the value plus one-fifth. The moment one picked up the shofar to blow it, he used it for his own benefit, thereby deconsecrating it. Therefore, he effectively blew a shofar that did not belong to the Temple and has fulfilled his obligation.

The *Shelamim* offering, however, is not subject to the law of *me'ilah*. Therefore, the shofar remained consecrated, and when he blew it, he was benefitting from Temple goods and he does not fulfill his obligation. Rava initially suggests that, even when one uses the *olah* shofar, he would not fulfill his obligation either, since the benefit of its use only accrues at the completion of the mitzvah. Thus, while he was blowing it, he doesn't yet have any benefit and so he's still using Temple goods.

Nevertheless, Rava concludes that in the case of both offerings, one has indeed fulfilled his obligation. Why? Because mitzvos were not given for the purpose of deriving benefit. One is not allowed to derive benefit from consecrated Temple property. Since doing a mitzvah, however, is not meant for personal enjoyment purposes, no deconsecration takes place when you perform the mitzvah of blowing the shofar with a sacrificial horn.

Rashi emphasizes this idea and notes that mitzvos were placed as a yoke upon our necks. A yoke is a bar placed on an animal attaching it to a load that it is required to pull. That's how we should treat our performance of mitzvos. As enjoyable as they might be, ultimately, we are doing them not to serve our own interests and pleasure but to serve Heaven.

That doesn't mean that your mitzvah observance should be devoid of pleasure. You should enjoy performing the will of Heaven. What it means is that it shouldn't be your sole motivation. When you're only doing mitzvos because of the fun factor, you'll prioritize those mitzvos that you enjoy and end up neglecting those mitzvos that you're not particularly excited about. Or, you'll fulfill the mitzvah in such a way that it comes easy to you and avoid any challenging aspects of the mitzvah.

For example, when it comes to hosting people in our homes, there are two types of guests: friends and true guests. We all like to be surrounded by our friends, and it's wonderful to keep company with good friends. But that's not the mitzvah of *hachnasas orchim*. The mitzvah is often mistranslated as "inviting guests." But it's easy to invite friends over to the house. The real mitzvah is when you "bring in" people who otherwise wouldn't be invited.

That's what Avraham and Sarah would do—open their tent to complete strangers. And they wouldn't just seat them at the end of the table with all the exciting conversation taking place at the head. They would serve them the finest delicacies and wait on their guests, meeting their every need—even washing their hands and feet!

For many decades, my in-laws (may they live and be well, till 120) were known in their neighborhood for their incredible hospitality. Every Shabbos, my father-in-law would bring home any number of people from shul that had no prior dinner plans. Consequently, their table was filled week-in, week-out, with the most beautiful *neshamos* that you could find. They were all such *tayere Yidden* (dear brothers and sisters), but each with a story. There were mature bachelors, widows with their orphan children, Yankele with the wooden leg, and, of course, the unfortunate souls who simply had nowhere else to be.

And then there were those times of year, around the Yomim Tovim, when their home was not only the best restaurant in town, but they opened their humble abode to wayfarers to stay over. Their generosity was so famous that the rooms would be wall-to-wall with sleeping bags.

One night, my father-in-law returned home late from the office. Not wishing to startle anyone, he knocked gently on the front door and pushed it open slowly. Most of the guests were fast asleep. All of a sudden, however, a head pops up and shouts out to him as he was doing his best to make his way across the room without stepping on anyone, "Sorry, sir, there's no more room here. You'll have to find another house!"

The Baal Shem Tov explains the practical application of our Sages' dictum, "Bringing in guests is greater than receiving the Divine presence." Bringing guests into one's home does not just entail physical and material effort; there are spiritual consequences too. Having guests means more than simply giving them a meal and a place to stay. We see from Avraham and Sarah the extent to which one must go to make a guest feel welcome. While nobody is expecting you to start washing their feet, bringing in guests nonetheless implies a real commitment to taking care of your guests—from seeking their welfare to making small-talk.

What sort of spiritual sacrifices is the Baal Shem Tov talking about? When all you want to do is finish your meal quickly and pick up your Gemara, the teaching of our Sages is activated. Now is not the time to "receive the Divine presence." Your guests' needs and comfort take precedence even over Hashem's requirements, so to speak.

And that's the meaning of doing mitzvos not for the sake of your personal pleasure and enjoyment. When you feel that your own schedule and life are being disturbed to help others, that's when it's clear that the mitzvah is a yoke upon your neck. It's a pure mitzvah when you've gone above and beyond your comfort zone.

Mitzvos are commandments. The Torah is not a menu from which we can pick and choose the activities we enjoy. May you accept the yoke of Heaven and nullify your will before His!

DAF 29

Finding a Life Coach

wo stories:

Story #1. Following the Exodus from Egypt, the army of Amalek attacked the Children of Israel. Moshe climbed to the top of the hill and raised his hands in prayer. Alongside him stood Aharon and Chur, each supporting one of his arms. They understood well the importance of their task, for should Moshe's hands become weak and drop down in fatigue, the Israelites would weaken before the Amalekite army.

Story #2. When the Israelites complained against God in the desert, He sent a plague of snakes against them. When the people realized their transgression, they repented and requested a cure to save them from their snake bites. Hashem told Moshe to build a structure consisting of the form of a serpent upon a pole. Whoever would gaze upon Moshe's serpent would survive.

מַתְנִי׳ וְהָיָה כַּאֲשֶׁר יָרִים מֹשֶׁה יָדוֹ וְגָבַר יִשְׂרָאֵל וְגוֹ׳ וְכִי יָדָיו שֶׁל מֹשֶׁה עוֹשׂוֹת
מִלְחָמָה אוֹ שׁוֹבְרוֹת מִלְחָמָה אֶלָּא לוֹמַר לְךָ כָּל זְמַן שֶׁהָיוּ יִשְׂרָאֵל מִסְתַּכְּלִין
כְּלַפֵּי מַעְלָה וּמְשַׁעְבְּדִין אֶת לִבָּם לַאֲבִיהֶם שֶׁבַּשָּׁמַיִם הָיוּ מִתְגַּבְּרִים וְאִם לָאו
הָיוּ נוֹפְלִים כַּיּוֹצֵא בַּדָּבָר אַתָּה אוֹמֵר עֲשֵׂה לְךָ שָׂרָף וְשִׂים אוֹתוֹ עַל נֵס וְהָיָה
כָּל הַנָּשׁוּךְ וְרָאָה אוֹתוֹ וָחָי וְכִי נָחָשׁ מֵמִית אוֹ נָחָשׁ מְחַיֶּה אֶלָּא בִּזְמַן שֶׁיִּשְׂרָאֵל
מִסְתַּכְּלִין כְּלַפֵּי מַעְלָה וּמְשַׁעְבְּדִין אֶת לִבָּם לַאֲבִיהֶם שֶׁבַּשָּׁמַיִם הָיוּ מִתְרַפְּאִין
וְאִם לָאו הָיוּ נִימוֹקִים.

99

"And when Moshe lifted his hands, Israel was more powerful..."
But do Moshe's hands make war or break war? Rather, the
Torah is teaching that as long as Israel would turn their gaze
Heavenward and subjugate their hearts to their Father in
Heaven, they would be empowered. Otherwise, they would fall.
Similarly, you find the following: "Make for yourself a serpent
and place it on a pole. Anyone who has been bitten shall see it
and live." Does a snake kill or does a snake give life? Rather, as
long as Israel turned their gaze Heavenward and subjugated
their hearts to their Father in Heaven, they would be healed.
Otherwise, they would perish.

What is the significance of Moshe's hands growing weak? Why did Aharon and Chur have to support him? The Talmud is imparting a powerful lesson about Moshe Rabbeinu as the leader and motivator of the people. Moshe's job was to point to the Heavens and remind people from where their salvation came. Every time they looked in his direction, they would see his hands in the air and pray to God for victory in battle.

Does a football team need a coach? Does an orchestra need a conductor? Strictly speaking, no they don't. But they can only continue for so long in the absence of the fellow standing in front directing them, before they stop working in sync and start losing their momentum and drive.

Throughout your life, you need to find yourself coaches, mentors, and motivators to keep you inspired and achieving your very best. We all run the risk of losing the spark or becoming unfocused without a coach to keep us on track. *Pirkei Avos* instructs us, "Make for yourself a teacher, and acquire for yourself a friend." An important role played by these teachers and friends is to always challenge you to be the very best that you can be. Your spiritual mentor is there to constantly remind you Who's in charge.

What's particularly noteworthy is the Torah's lesson that even the greatest motivator doesn't possess limitless wellsprings of vigor. Even a Moshe Rabbeinu grows weary, and that's why he needed support from his friends too. If you've merited to be placed in a leadership position, don't think that you can go on forever without any support and assistance. You'll grow weary along the way. But that's OK. As long as you have the right support in place, you'll be able to rest a little while they hold down the fort, and then you can continue to motivate the team to achieve greatness.

How about the serpent on the pole? Rabbi Samson Raphael Hirsch explains that the purpose of the serpent image was to remind the people why they were praying to God when they looked up.[1] Think about the prevalence of snakes in the desert as the Israelites sojourned through. Naturally, snake attacks should have been an everyday occurrence. The fact that they were not attacked regularly was on account of Hashem's protection. Once they sinned by complaining, the Almighty temporarily removed His special protection and allowed the snakes to engage in their natural offensive behavior.

The snake that Moshe raised and instructed the people to gaze at served as a reminder of all the "snakes" that seek to bite us all day, every day. If you only knew all the occasions that the Almighty intervenes to keep you safe and secure, you'd constantly be raising your eyes Heavenward and thanking Him. Your success is just as much due to the Almighty removing the stumbling blocks and attackers, as it is your personal efforts. Part of the task of the spiritual motivator is to remind you constantly to acknowledge not only God's help, but also His removal of all obstacles to your success.

Find good mentors in life. A good coach will point you in the right direction, remind you where your strength comes from and make sure you stay on track to achieve your goals. May you find the right people to become your very best!

---

1   *Bamidbar* 21:8.

If at First You Don't Succeed

O ur patriarch Avraham wasn't always a believer in monotheism. He grew up in the home of Terach, a well-known idol merchant. Already as a young child, however, Avraham recognized the falsehood of idolatry. He looked to the sky and saw the sun, the great provider of light and warmth to the world. "That must be the ultimate god," he said to himself. But then the sun was replaced in the sky by the moon. Unlike the sun, the moon seemed to never disappear.

Avraham would often notice the moon watching over the Earth even during the daylight hours. "Aha, that must be the ultimate God," he thought. But then the moon would slowly shrink until it disappeared each month. So, Avraham concluded that the moon couldn't be the ultimate god either. Finally, he decided that there must be an invisible God that rules over everything in the universe; that God was constantly present.

Avraham was so filled with passion about his new discovery that the next day he went and smashed all the idols in his father's shop. Incensed, his father took him to King Nimrod to stand trial. Avraham was convicted of rebellion against the gods and thrown into a fiery furnace. Miraculously, he escaped unscathed. Nevertheless, from that moment on, his approach to persuading others of the truth of monotheism was radically different. No longer would he resort to violent measures to prove his point. Avraham learned that reaching out to

others in kindness was the best way to demonstrate the truth of his
religious beliefs.

מַתְנִי׳ בָּרִאשׁוֹנָה הָיוּ מְקַבְּלִין עֵדוּת הַחֹדֶשׁ כָּל הַיּוֹם וּפַעַם אַחַת נִשְׁתַּהוּ
הָעֵדִים מִלָּבוֹא וְנִתְקַלְקְלוּ הַלְוִיִּם בַּשִּׁיר הִתְקִינוּ שֶׁלֹּא יְהוּ מְקַבְּלִין אֶלָּא עַד
הַמִּנְחָה וְאִם בָּאוּ עֵדִים מִן הַמִּנְחָה וּלְמַעְלָה נוֹהֲגִין אוֹתוֹ הַיּוֹם קוֹדֶשׁ וּלְמָחָר
קוֹדֶשׁ מִשֶּׁחָרַב בֵּית הַמִּקְדָּשׁ הִתְקִין רַבָּן יוֹחָנָן בֶּן זַכַּאי שֶׁיְּהוּ מְקַבְּלִין עֵדוּת
הַחֹדֶשׁ כָּל הַיּוֹם: גְּמ׳ מָה קִלְקוּל קִלְקְלוּ הַלְוִיִּם בַּשִּׁיר הָכָא תַּרְגִּימוּ שֶׁלֹּא
אָמְרוּ שִׁירָה כָּל עִיקָּר רַבִּי זֵירָא אָמַר שֶׁאָמְרוּ שִׁירָה שֶׁל חוֹל עִם תָּמִיד שֶׁל
בֵּין הָעַרְבַּיִם אָמַר לוֹ רַבִּי זֵירָא לְאַהֲבָה בְּרֵיהּ פּוֹק תְּנִי לְהוּ הִתְקִינוּ שֶׁלֹּא יְהוּ
מְקַבְּלִין עֵדוּת הַחֹדֶשׁ אֶלָּא כְּדֵי שֶׁיְּהֵא שָׁהוּת בַּיּוֹם לְהַקְרִיב תְּמִידִין וּמוּסָפִין
וְנִסְכֵּיהֶם וְלוֹמַר שִׁירָה שֶׁלֹּא בְּשִׁיבּוּשׁ אִי אָמְרַתְּ בִּשְׁלָמָא אָמוּר שִׁירָה דְחוֹל
הַיְינוּ דְאִיכָּא שִׁיבּוּשׁ אֶלָּא אִי אָמְרַתְּ לָא אָמוּר כְּלָל מַאי שִׁיבּוּשׁ אִיכָּא כֵּיוָן
דְלָא אָמוּר כְּלָל אֵין לְךָ שִׁיבּוּשׁ גָּדוֹל מִזֶּה.

*Mishnah: Initially, they would accept testimony to determine
the start of the month throughout the entire thirtieth day.
Once, the witnesses tarried in coming, and the Levites erred
with regard to the song. From that point on, the Sages instituted that they would accept testimony to determine the start
of the month only until Minchah time. And if witnesses came
from Minchah time onward, they would observe that day as
sacred, and they would also observe the following day as sacred. After the Temple was destroyed, Rabban Yochanan ben
Zakkai instituted that they would once again accept testimony
to determine the start of the month the entire day.*

*Gemara: What error did the Levites make with regard to the
song? Here, in Babylonia, they interpreted that they did not
recite any song at all. Rabbi Zeira said: They recited the song of
an ordinary weekday with the daily afternoon offering. Rabbi
Zeira said to his son Ahavah: Go out and teach: They instituted
that the court would accept testimony to determine the start of
the month only if there was enough time left in the day to sacrifice the daily offerings and the additional offerings and their
libations, and to recite the song without a mistake. Granted, if
you say that they recited the song of an ordinary weekday, this*

> *is a case in which there is a mistake. However, if you say that*
> *they did not recite any song at all, what mistake is there? Since*
> *they did not recite any song at all, you do not have a mistake*
> *greater than this.*

In ancient times, the monthly calendar was determined according to the sighting of the new moon. The lunar cycle is approximately 29½ days, and so a month consists of either 29 or 30 days. If the witnesses appeared on the day after the 29th, that day became the first of the new month, and hence the previous month had 29 days. If not, then inevitably, that day would be the 30th of the old month and the next day became the 1st of the new month. On most months of the year, it was immaterial what time during the 30th day the witnesses arrived. Whenever they appeared and had their testimony validated, that day that was previously considered the 30th of the old month would be transformed into the first of the new month, leaving the previous month as a 29-day month.

One month of the year, however, is more complicated. On the first of Tishrei, we celebrate Rosh Hashanah, and so, if the witnesses only arrived late in the day, the Temple service would be affected: If today is Rosh Chodesh (the first of the new month), then today is also Rosh Hashanah, and we have not performed the correct service and haven't sung the right song of the day in the Temple!

What did they do? In Babylonia, the Rabbis explained that the Levites would not sing any song that day. On the one hand, they reasoned that the witnesses might arrive, and so they didn't want to sing the song of the weekday. On the other hand, in the absence of witnesses, they couldn't sing the song of the Rosh Hashanah festival. Therefore, they didn't sing any song at all.

Rabbi Zeira demurs. He suggests that they did in fact sing the song of the weekday. He offers a *Beraisa* as proof for his position. "The rabbis instituted that they would not accept testimony of the new month unless there was enough time left in the day to offer the various sacrifices of Rosh Hashanah and to chant the song *without a mistake.*"

Asks Rabbi Zeira, "It makes sense if you say that they sang the weekday song, hence they erred. But if you say that they had not sung anything, then what was the error?"

The Rabbis respond, "There is no greater mistake than not singing anything at all."

There are various reasons why people fail at achieving success and making their dreams come true, but, the number one reason, says the Gemara, is simply this: People are afraid of failure, and so they do not even set out and make the effort to accomplish and be what they dream to be. That's the meaning of the Rabbis' declaration: "There is no greater mistake than not singing at all."

Did you know that for every scientific breakthrough, hundreds of laboratory tests fail? But without experimentation, that one successful discovery could never happen. In other words, before that wonder drug was created, the scientists who produced it would go into work each day and fail. Can you imagine how that must feel? To come home each day knowing that all your efforts were for naught. And, yet, without all those efforts, it would be impossible to achieve the ultimate success of the breakthrough. That's why the greatest mistake is not singing at all. Without that effort and willingness to try and fail, no success would ever be achieved.

Have you ever embarked on a community program, only to be disappointed when the numbers weren't as strong as you anticipated? That's a step toward success. Of course, you could put on a program that was run-of-the-mill that your regular twenty-five people would show up to. But if you want hundreds of attendees, that requires creativity and experimentation. It's not always going to work. Sometimes you're going to invest a lot into an initiative that just won't pan out. But successful companies do that all the time. They have a line item on their budget dedicated to failure. It's called R&D—research and development. Without it, they would never become better; they would remain mediocre and lackluster.

That's the attitude that we need to strive for throughout our lives. Whether it's our communal life, professional life, or personal life, without taking risks and knowing that failure is inevitable, we won't achieve the incredible successes that are destined for us.

Shlomo HaMelech famously wrote, "The *tzaddik* will fall seven times and rise."[1] That's a powerful declaration. Based upon this, it's possible to say that for every time you hope to succeed, it will take seven prior failures. The good news is that you now have the formula, so you can start counting. If you've experienced a failure in life, you're one-seventh of the way toward success. Only six more failed tries to go, and you'll be well on the way to achieving your dreams. For some, those failures will be in the realm of business ventures. For others, it will be relationships that don't work out. For others still, it will be medical treatments that have only a small chance of success. We all have areas of our life where we want to thrive. The key is never to give up and settle for mediocre effort and keeping things on an even keel.

Even our forefather Avraham didn't get it right the first time. First it was sun-worship. Then moon-worship. Then idol-smashing. Only after all of these failed experiments did he realize that serving the one God in a way that brought joy and positivity into people's lives was the right path. Avraham would never have reached that realization had he not taken risks and experimented with his initial ideas.

Very rarely does anyone succeed on the first try. Take those risks. Sing that song. It's OK to fail and sing the wrong song. In fact, failure is not just OK; it's a prerequisite to success. May you accept failure with grace, knowing that every failure is a step closer to the ultimate success of that which you dream of in your life!

---

1   *Mishlei* 24:16.

DAF 31

Visiting an Aquarium Is a Mitzvah

R abbi Meir was once challenged by a non-observant neighbor, who demanded proof for God's existence.

"This world just happened to come into existence by accident," he claimed defiantly. Rabbi Meir did not respond.

The following Shabbos, Rabbi Meir invited the man over for lunch. After the meal, the man rose from the table and looked around the room. On the wall was the most beautiful painting of the Mediterranean coast.

"Who is the artist of this masterpiece?" the neighbor inquired.

"Funny you should ask," replied Rabbi Meir. "Just the other day, I had a paint palate on my desk when the cat jumped up and knocked it over. I couldn't believe my eyes when I discovered the picture that resulted. That's the painting before your eyes!"

"What nonsense are you speaking?" said the man with a shaking of his head. "A picture so beautiful could only have been made by an accomplished artist."

"Aha!" Rabbi Meir responded. "If a simple painting on canvas could not have happened by accident, then take a look at our intricate and colorful world. Do you really believe it happened by accident?"

רַבִּי יְהוּדָה אוֹמֵר מִשׁוּם רַבִּי עֲקִיבָא בַּחֲמִישִׁי הָיוּ אוֹמְרִים הַרְנִינוּ לֵאלֹקִים עוּזֵנוּ עַל שֵׁם שֶׁבָּרָא עוֹפוֹת וְדָגִים לְשַׁבֵּחַ לִשְׁמוֹ.

רש"י: שברא עופות ודגים לשבח לשמו—כשאדם רואה עופות משונים זה מזה נותן שבח למי שבראם.

107

Rabbi Yehudah quoted Rabbi Akiva: On the fifth day of the week, the Levites would recite the psalm: "Sing aloud to God, our strength," because on the fifth day of Creation He created birds and fish to praise His name.

Rashi: When a person sees a variety of birds, he gives praise to the One who created them.

Have you ever wondered why God created all types of weird and wonderful species of fish, fowl, and beasts? What purpose do they serve?

Every day of the week, we recite a different Psalm that was originally chanted by the Levites in the Holy Temple. This is called the Song of the Day. The Psalm for Thursday, the fifth day, was designated in praise of the Almighty who made the birds and the fish on the fifth day of creation. When a person sees the multitude of different species of birds and fish, one is inspired to offer praise to the One who created them.

On a recent visit to Australia, we were walking along the pier at Darling Harbour.

"Should we take the kids to the Sydney Aquarium?" I asked Batya.

"Sounds great!" the Rabbanit responded.

I went inside to purchase tickets and walked out five minutes later with a huge frown.

"It's over a hundred dollars for all of us!" I exclaimed.

"It's worth it," replied Batya. "After all, it's a mitzvah!"

If Hashem has created different kinds of fish, then it is incumbent upon us to seek them out and become awestruck by their beauty. The Almighty fashioned all these creatures in order that we should marvel at the expanse of creation and be inspired to praise Him.

Taking the kids to an aquarium isn't just another way to keep them occupied. Don't think of it as another day in another amusement park. Visiting the aquarium is a mitzvah so long as you utilize your time there properly and make it a spiritual experience. Next time you take the family to a zoo or aquarium, don't just teach them the *what* of the animals. Teach them the *why* of the animals. They were placed in this world to inspire us to praise our Creator!

We're all familiar with the three steps of prayer: praise, request, and thanks. An essential element of connecting with the Almighty is praise. Praise doesn't happen in a vacuum. In order to praise Hashem, we often require external stimuli.

For some, that might be a beautiful sunset. For others, it's the sights and sounds of a nature walk, or it's a look up at the stars in the sky. These experiences could be self-serving—merely to satisfy one's own desire for pleasure and enjoyment—or, they could be vehicles of inspiration for praising Heaven.

Why is praise an integral part of Jewish prayer? Because *tefillah* is not just about asking God for our needs. It's about communicating with Him. It's about creating a connection with Him. That's what praise achieves. When you "give" something to God, you grow closer to Him. And sometimes you need to seek experiences that will fill you with praises for Him.

This universe is extraordinary. Take a good look at the wonders of Creation and develop your relationship with the Creator. May you be forever inspired to praise and bond with Him!

DAF 32

Your Butterfly Effect Is Eternal

Ruth was a Moabite. Married to the son of Elimelech and Naomi, she was widowed young. Another woman would have accepted her lot and bid farewell to the family to start life afresh. But not Ruth. She looked at her poor, aging mother-in-law and decided that she would take it upon herself to be there for her every step of the way.

They made their way back to the Land of Israel, where Ruth went out to work on the threshing floor to make ends meet and provide for and take care of Naomi. Eventually, God rewarded Ruth for her extraordinary kindness and brought her a new husband, Boaz.

What's more, Ruth merited having a book of *Tanach* named in her honor. The book concludes with the story of Boaz and Ruth's offspring. "Boaz fathered Oved, Oved fathered Yishai, and Yishai fathered David." From Ruth, the mother of kings, came David HaMelech, from whom will come Mashiach.

בְּרֹאשׁ הַשָּׁנָה לֵיכָּא הַלֵּל מַאי טַעְמָא אָמַר רַבִּי אַבָּהוּ אָמְרוּ מַלְאֲכֵי הַשָּׁרֵת לִפְנֵי הַקָּדוֹשׁ בָּרוּךְ הוּא רִבּוֹנוֹ שֶׁל עוֹלָם מִפְּנֵי מָה אֵין יִשְׂרָאֵל אוֹמְרִים שִׁירָה לְפָנֶיךָ בְּרֹאשׁ הַשָּׁנָה וּבְיוֹם הַכִּפּוּרִים אָמַר לָהֶם אֶפְשָׁר מֶלֶךְ יוֹשֵׁב עַל כִּסֵּא דִין וְסִפְרֵי חַיִּים וְסִפְרֵי מֵתִים פְּתוּחִין לְפָנָיו וְיִשְׂרָאֵל אוֹמְרִים שִׁירָה.

On Rosh Hashanah, there is no recitation of Hallel. What is the reason? Rabbi Avahu said: The ministering angels said before the Holy One, blessed be He: "Master of the Universe,

110

for what reason don't the Jewish People recite songs of praise before You on Rosh Hashanah and on Yom Kippur?" He said to them: "Is it possible that while the King is sitting on the throne of judgment and the books of the living (chaim) and the books of the dead (meisim) are open before Him, the Jewish People are chanting songs?"

On the *Yamim Nora'im*, we ask Hashem to write us in the "Book of *Chaim*." We usually translate this prayer as a request to be inscribed in the "Book of Life." But, as we see here in the Gemara, the word *chaim* stands in contradistinction to the word *meisim*, which means "deceased." In other words, the Almighty has two sets of books in front of Him—books judging those who are alive and books judging those who have passed on.

How are the deceased judged? They haven't performed any mitzvos over the course of the last twelve months!

During our life on Earth, our souls grow with every mitzvah that we do. But, once we've passed on to the Next World, we are helpless in terms of our accomplishments and growth potential. We can no longer grow, since being in the World of Truth where everything is clear, we no longer have free choice.

How does a soul achieve elevation in the Next World? Through the actions of his relatives and others whom he impacted during his lifetime on Earth. He is judged by the consequences of his actions during his time on earth as they play out each year.

Everything we do, every step we take, has a butterfly effect that reverberates for all eternity. The more positive influence we have during our lifetimes, the greater our eternal reward will be, as that reward builds on itself year after year after year.

Just think: Every time you influence someone to become more engaged in his Yiddishkeit, you are impacting not only him but his children and his children's children and so on for generations to come. After you pass on to the Next World, your merits will continue to accrue. Each year, the Almighty opens your book—one of the Books of the Deceased—and looks at how your lifetime actions continue to impact the world. He then judges you accordingly. With the positive influence you've kick-started, you're on your way to elevation upon elevation, soaring through the spiritual heights for all eternity!

But now, let's flip the equation and work backward. The fact that you are reading this piece of Torah is a consequence of a combination of a number of people who came before you and brought you to this point. The Torah that you are learning is not only a merit for you, but a merit accruing toward their spiritual bank accounts as well. Some of those individuals are still living, others have passed on. Either way, their souls are growing in merit on account of your mitzvah.

That's one of the reasons why you begin your thrice-daily *Amidah* prayer appealing to "our God, and the God of our parents, the God of Avraham, the God of Yitzchak, and the God of Yaakov." All the generations going back all the way to our patriarchs and matriarchs are all affected by your actions. So, you can imagine how they're rooting for your spiritual success. Your decisions will impact not just yourself and your descendants but also all your forebears!

Ruth's acts of kindness won the heart of Boaz. But they achieved much more than that. They led to the birth of the great David HaMelech and the ensuing Davidic dynasty—from kings to Rabbinic leaders—throughout our history. Every spiritual success that they've enjoyed has been a boost—an elevation—for Ruth along her spiritual journey, until this very day.

Every step in this world has infinite reach. May you always consider the consequences of every thought, speech, and action, not just upon yourself but upon all who preceded and are destined to succeed you!

Who Are We
Unwittingly Damaging?

After being led into Canaan under the leadership of Yehoshua, the Children of Israel have been living in the Promised Land for some time, but many areas remain in the hands of the Canaanites. The time is now ripe to drive out Sisera's army from their midst. Devorah, the prophetess and judge of the people, calls upon Barak, and instructs him to take the men out to battle. "I shall only go if you accompany me," he replies.

Sure enough, the Israelites vanquish the Canaanite army. Sisera, however, escapes from the battlefield and seeks a hiding place to disappear until he can escape. He chances upon the tent of Yael and asks her to hide him. Yael invites him in, but then, after lulling him to sleep, ends his life.

Following the great victory, Devorah sings a song of thanksgiving. In her song, she highlights how Sisera would not be returning home from the battlefield that day.

"Through the window, the mother of Sisera looked forth and wept by the portal. 'Why does his chariot tarry, why are the hoof sounds delayed?'"

אָמַר אַבָּיֵי כְּתִיב יוֹם תְּרוּעָה יִהְיֶה לָכֶם וּמְתַרְגְּמִינַן יוֹם יַבָּבָא יְהֵא לְכוֹן וּכְתִיב בְּאִימֵיהּ דְּסִיסְרָא בְּעַד הַחַלּוֹן נִשְׁקְפָה וַתְּיַבֵּב אֵם סִיסְרָא.

Abaye said: It is written: "It shall be a day of sounding the shofar (teruah) for you," and we translate this verse as: It is a day of yevava to you. Concerning the meaning of the word yevavah, it is written about the mother of Sisera: "Through the window the mother of Sisera looked forth and wept [va'teyabev]."

Concerning Rosh Hashanah, the Torah says, "It shall be a day of *teruah* (blowing) for you." *Onkelos* translates the word *teruah* as *yevavah*. Finding the same word *yevavah* employed to describe the weeping of Sisera's mother, Abaye demonstrates that the *teruah* blast should sound like a person weeping.

Sometimes in life, there are battles to be fought. Some of these take place on a national level, others on a personal level. The song of Devorah offers us a profound insight into the way we must go to war and deal with those on the other side of the battlefield. Most armies train their soldiers to view those on the other side of the battlefield as less than human.

That's not our approach. When Devorah sings her victory song, she takes a moment to think about Sisera, albeit her enemy, but also a fellow human being. True, we had to stop him dead in his tracks so that we wouldn't be destroyed, but we take a moment to remember that even Sisera, no doubt, has a family waiting for him back home. The consequences of his death have an impact way beyond his individual physical space.

War is not pretty. Sometimes it's necessary, but, says Devorah, let's not glorify it. The casualties of the battle—far and wide—are innumerable. It's easy to dismiss the "other" when we demonize them and treat them as mere objects. Devorah teaches us to view everyone, first and foremost, as fellow human beings—to remembers that they are husbands, wives, fathers, mothers, spouses, sons, daughters, and siblings, and that whatever happens now is going to impact many other people who are not present right here and now.

Of course, we must be concerned for the casualties of battles and disputes that take place, not only on a grand national and international level, but throughout our lives. Maybe you have a work colleague that you've upset. You tell yourself that it's no big deal, they'll get over it. But then they go home and let out their frustration on their spouse or children.

Or, perhaps, you've allowed someone to be embarrassed publicly. You figure that the person deserved the way that he was treated. But we forget that the person has a spouse and children who are also going to suffer embarrassment on account of the incident. We have to be so careful and think about the repercussions—not only for present company, but for any innocents who might be collateral damage from our behavior.

The Israeli Defense Force prides itself on being the most moral army in the world. When it wants to attack Hamas, it first air-drops leaflets warning people to clear out of the area so that there won't be innocent casualties. May you always give great consideration to the reverberations of all your actions and to everyone who might be impacted by your decisions!

Facing God

One of the first things that a parent does on a Friday night is to bless his children with the priestly benediction:

"May Hashem bless you and guard you. May Hashem shine His face toward you and favor you. May Hashem turn His face toward you and grant you peace."

Why do we offer the blessing at that time of the week in particular? Why do we offer that particular blessing? What is the meaning of Hashem's face?

תְּקִיעוֹת וּבְרָכוֹת שֶׁל רֹאשׁ הַשָּׁנָה וְשֶׁל יוֹם הַכִּפּוּרִים מְעַכְּבוֹת מַאי טַעְמָא אָמַר רַבָּה אָמַר הַקָּדוֹשׁ בָּרוּךְ הוּא אִמְרוּ לְפָנַי בְּרֹאשׁ הַשָּׁנָה מַלְכִיּוֹת זִכְרוֹנוֹת וְשׁוֹפָרוֹת מַלְכִיּוֹת כְּדֵי שֶׁתַּמְלִיכוּנִי עֲלֵיכֶם זִכְרוֹנוֹת כְּדֵי שֶׁיָּבֹא לְפָנַי זִכְרוֹנֵיכֶם לְטוֹבָה וּבַמֶּה בְּשׁוֹפָר.

The shofar blasts and blessings of Rosh Hashanah and Yom Kippur invalidate one another. What is the reason? Rabbah said that the Holy One, blessed be He, said: "Recite before Me (lefanai) on Rosh Hashanah Kingship, Remembrances, and Shofaros. Kingship, so that you will crown Me as King over you; Remembrances, so that your remembrance will rise before Me (lefanai) for good. And with what? With the shofar."

Rabbi Levi Yitzchak of Berditchev notes that the word *lefanai* literally means "to My face." He explains that, according to Kabbalah, the face represents the Divine will to shower blessing upon us. Rabbah is teaching that to crown God means to seek a face-to-face, direct relationship with Him. We are telling the Almighty that we are ready to make Him ever-present in our lives. At that point, replies Hashem, our remembrances—our merits—appear right before His face, and He opens up His storehouse of blessing for us.[1]

When we evoke Hashem's "face" in our prayers, it's all about having a direct, continuous relationship with Him. In the Yom Tov *duchening* (the service of the priestly blessing), there are certain verses that appear in the siddur alongside each word explaining the *kavanah* of the word. Next to the word for "His face," the verse from *Tehillim* reads, "Turn to me and favor me, for I am alone and deprived." In other words, when we seek the blessing of Hashem's face, we seek His undivided attention.

Of course, Hashem always gives us His undivided attention. The problem is that we don't appreciate it, because we're preoccupied with other matters. Hearing about Hashem turning His face to us and focusing completely on us, we are motivated to improve our focus on Him. How do we do that?

While technological advances are meant to make our lives better, often times, they are unfortunately detrimental to our relationships and ourselves. Remember the days when, if you had something to say, you'd pick up the phone and have a conversation? Nowadays, it's all text and email. Technology is so advanced that we don't need to talk to anyone anymore.

What's the one piece of technology that has improved relationships? Facetime and Zoom now allow you to talk to another person and see that person in real-time. That's actually even better than the telephone. Why? When people talk on the phone, you never really know if you have their undivided attention. They might be watching TV, reading the newspaper, or checking email. You often feel that they might not quite be with you, but you don't know for sure. With Facetime, suddenly you have to give the other person your undivided attention. Now that's

---

1   *Kedushas Levi, Nitzavim.*

an improvement in interpersonal relationships for the twenty-first century!

Facetime and Zoom teach us a powerful lesson about how we interact with others and what a direct face-to-face relationship with Hashem might look like. If you want Hashem's camera on, if you want Him unmuted, then you need to turn your camera on and unmute yourself. Your relationship with Him must be "on" constantly and never distracted by other matters while He is "lecturing" in the background.

That's why you start Shabbos with the priestly benediction. You are telling your children that while the week may have been incredibly busy—running here and there, working long hours, attending to various commitments—on Shabbos, you are devoted to giving them Facetime, i.e., your undivided attention. You are promising them that the next twenty-five hours won't be about catching up on the Times or even *daf yomi*. It won't be about hanging out with your shul buddies, talking sports, and politics. Shabbos is about family.

May you always keep your relationship with God and your loved ones at the front of your mind and your life, and may He shower you with His blessing!

DAF 35

Ready to Pray

The story is told of Reb Zundel who goes to the Baal Shem Tov, the founder of the Chassidic movement, and asks for advice on how to pray. The Rebbe responds, "If you vow to always read your prayers from the siddur, never praying by heart, your prayers will be immeasurably changed." And so Zundel did. From that day on, he made sure to always carry a pocket siddur on him so that, come what may, he could read the words of the prayers.

One day, Reb Zundel, who was a furrier, was on a business trip when his wagon was crossing a bridge. Suddenly the rope snapped, the bridge gave way, and Zundel managed to jump out of the wagon just in time to save himself. Swimming to shore, he found himself bereft of all his belongings, including thousands of rubles worth of furs.

"It's all in the Almighty's hands," Zundel thought to himself, "Thank God I survived unscathed." He then headed toward the main road to try to hitch a ride back home.

It was quite the walk, and he realized that the day was wearing on and he had not yet davened *Minchah*.

"Oy vey!" he cried. "My siddur is at the bottom of the river!"

Nu, what choice did he have? This would have to be the first time since the Rebbe's instruction that he would need to pray by heart. It wouldn't be a major problem; after all, he had been uttering the same prayers for decades.

"But I made a promise!" he thought to himself, and he decided that he would devise a plan to pray from the text.

He was still wandering through the woods when he arrived at a beautiful, big house. He knocked on the door, and a finely-attired gentleman answered. Unbeknownst to Zundel, this man was the local squire.

"Can I help you?" he asked.

"Please, sir," replied Reb Zundel, "all I am looking for is a pen and a piece of paper. And, I promise, I won't bother you any further."

Bemused by the strange request, the squire handed Zundel the pen and paper and offered him a table to write.

"Are you writing a letter to a loved one?" the squire asked curiously.

"No," said Zundel. He explained to the squire about the vow he had made years earlier, and he proceeded to write down the entire *Minchah* service so that he could pray from the text.

The squire watched Reb Zundel from the moment his pen connected with the paper until he finally finished his prayers, awestruck by this man of God.

"What do you do and what brought you here?" inquired the squire. Zundel told him all about his sales trip, the collapsed bridge, and his lost wares and siddur.

"Zundel," said the squire, "today is your lucky day. I am setting off tomorrow morning to visit the prince to arrange local business matters. How about you come with me and we can establish you as the official furrier for the province?"

אָמַר רַבִּי אֶלְעָזָר לְעוֹלָם יַסְדִּיר אָדָם תְּפִלָּתוֹ וְאַחַר כָּךְ יִתְפַּלֵּל.

Rabbi Elazar taught: A person should always arrange his prayers and subsequently pray.

Imagine you had an appointment to see the queen or the president. You would prepare at great length for the meeting. You'd make sure that you knew exactly what you were going to say, word for word, that your suit was finely pressed, and that you had prepared yourself mentally for the occasion.

And yet, when we are about to talk to the Supreme King of Kings, some of us casually stroll into the conversation. We need to prepare ourselves to pray. The Talmud teaches that pious people would meditate about God for an hour before they would pray. Some of us don't even think about Him for five minutes prior to picking up the siddur.

Sometimes we arrive late to shul, and so we say a few prayers and then skip to where the minyan is up to. The *Ben Ish Chai* notes that Rabbi Elazar instructs us to "arrange" our prayers in order. Reciting the prayers in order is important, he explains, because each section corresponds to a spiritual realm. According to Kabbalah, there are four divine worlds. The preliminary prayers about the sacrifices correspond to the supernal world of *Asiyah*. The next section of *Pesukei D'zimrah* corresponds to the world of *Yetzirah*. The *Shema* and its blessings correspond to *Beriah*, and the *Amidah* corresponds to *Atzilus*. One cannot simply skip from the physical realm to the upper worlds. It's a progression, without which the climactic *Amidah* prayer is lacking the spiritual fuel to make it effective.[1]

For some, arranging the prayers will mean always ensuring that the prayer service is recited meticulously in order. For others, preparation entails meditation and mindfulness prior to davening. Like the pious people of yore, they will think deeply about the sacred task they are about to embark upon. And for others, it will simply mean attending a *shiur* prior to davening. Having a mind focused on Torah is an excellent way to ready oneself for prayer.

Prayer is a serious endeavor. It's not something that we can just jump into. Just like any serious matters in our lives, if we seek to maximize productivity, we need to prepare for our prayers. Davening each word from the siddur is an excellent way to stay focused, and it makes a world of difference.

At the front of many shuls is the aphorism, "Know before Whom you are standing." That line serves as a constant reminder to stay focused on our conversation with the Almighty. May you always "arrange" your prayers. You will find that your ability to pray and find meaning in that part of your day will increase a thousand-fold!

---

1   *Ben Yehoyada.*

About the Author

Rabbi Daniel Friedman is currently on his fourth *daf yomi* cycle. He received *semichah yadin yadin* from Rav Gedalia Dov Schwartz, *zt"l*, Av Beis Din of the Beth Din of America. He has served communities in the US, Canada, Australia, and the UK. His articles have appeared in the *Journal of Halacha and Contemporary Society*, *YU Lamdan*, the *Jewish Press*, the *Jerusalem Post*, Aish.com, and numerous other outlets. He was the inaugural chair of the National Holocaust Monument of Canada and is a world-renowned expert on the intersection of halachah and international relations.

MOSAICA PRESS

BOOK PUBLISHERS

Elegant, Meaningful & Bold

info@MosaicaPress.com
www.MosaicaPress.com

The Mosaica Press team of
acclaimed editors and designers
is attracting some of the most
compelling thinkers and teachers
in the Jewish community today.
Our books are available around
the world.

HARAV YAACOV HABER
RABBI DORON KORNBLUTH